THE PARABLES OF JESUS THE MESSIAH

THE PARABLES OF JESUS THE MESSIAH

E. KEITH HOWICK

BOOKCRAFT
Salt Lake City, Utah

Library of Congress Catalog Card Number: 86-71660
ISBN 0-88494-608-8

First Printing, 1986

Printed in the United States of America

To Gail and Deni

Key to Abbreviations

Abbreviation	Name of Work
Armstrong	Edward A. Armstrong, *The Gospel Parables* (New York: Sheed and Ward, 1967).
Barclay	William Barclay, *And Jesus Said, A Handbook on the Parables of Jesus* (Philadelphia, Pennsylvania: The Westminster Press, 1970).
Barnett	Albert E. Barnett, *Understanding the Parables of Our Lord* (Nashville, Tennessee: Cokesbury Press, 1940).
Bruce	Alexander Balmain Bruce, *A Systematic and Critical Study of the Parables of Our Lord,* 7th ed. (London: Hodder and Stoughton, 1897).
Buttrick	George A. Buttrick, *The Parables of Jesus* (Grand Rapids, Michigan: Baker Book House, 1981).
Cadman	Samuel Parkes Cadman, D.D., *The Parables of Jesus* (Philadelphia, Pennsylvania: David McKay Company, 1931).
DNTC	Bruce R. McConkie, *Doctrinal New Testament Commentary,* Vol. 1, The Gospels, (Salt Lake City: Bookcraft, 1975).
Dodd	C. H. Dodd, *The Parables of the Kingdom* (New York: Charles Scribner's Sons, 1961).
EB	*Encyclopedia Britannica,* 15th ed. (Chicago: Encyclopedia Brittanica, Inc., 1978).
Ed	Alfred Edersheim, *The Life and Times of Jesus the Messiah,* reprint ed. (Grand Rapids, Michigan: William E. Eerdmans Publishing Co., 1981).

Ed(JSL)	Alfred Edersheim, *Sketches of Jewish Social Life in the Days of Christ* (Grand Rapids, Michigan: William B. Eerdmans Publishing Company, 1982).
Ed(Temple)	Alfred Edersheim, *The Temple: Its Ministry and Services as They Were at the Time of Jesus Christ,* reprint ed. (Grand Rapids, Michigan: William B. Eerdmans Publishing Company, 1982).
Farrar	Frederic W. Farrar, *The Life of Christ,* 2 vols. (New York: E. P. Dutton & Company, 1874).
Filas	Francis L. Filas, *The Parables of Jesus, A Popular Explanation* (New York: The Macmillan Company, 1959).
FPM	Spencer W. Kimball, *Faith Precedes the Miracle* (Salt Lake City: Deseret Book, 1972).
Geikie	Cunningham Geikie, *The Life and Words of Christ,* revised ed., 2 vols. (New York: Appleton & Company, 1891, 1894).
HC	Joseph Smith, Jr., *History of the Church of Jesus Christ of Latter-day Saints,* ed. B. H. Roberts, 7 vols. (Salt Lake City: The Church of Jesus Christ of Latter-day Saints, 1949).
JC	James E. Talmage, *Jesus the Christ* (Salt Lake City: Deseret Book, 1959).
Jeremias	Joachim Jeremias, *The Parables of Jesus,* revised ed. (New York: Charles Scribner's Sons, 1963).
Josephus	*Complete Works,* trans. Wm. Whiston (Grand Rapids, Michigan: Kregel Publications, 1971).
Miracles	E. Keith Howick, *The Miracles of Jesus the Messiah* (Salt Lake City: Bookcraft, 1985).

MF	Spencer W. Kimball, *The Miracle of Forgiveness* (Salt Lake City: Bookcraft, 1969).
MM	Bruce R. McConkie, *The Mortal Messiah,* 4 vols. (Salt Lake City: Deseret Book, 1979–1981).
PM	Bruce R. McConkie, *The Promised Messiah, The First Coming of Christ* (Salt Lake City: Deseret Book, 1978).
Smith	Joseph Fielding Smith, *The Way to Perfection* (Salt Lake City: Deseret Book, 1972).
Strauss	David Friedrich Strauss, *The Life of Jesus,* trans. George Eliot (London: Messrs. George Allen & Company, Ltd., 1906).
Tennyson	Alfred, Lord Tennyson, *Idylls of the King and a Selection of Poems* (New York: A Signet Classic, The New American Library, Inc., 1961).
TG	*Topical Guide* (Salt Lake City: The Church of Jesus Christ of Latter-day Saints, 1979).
TPJS	*Teachings of the Prophet Joseph Smith,* selected and arranged by Joseph Fielding Smith, Jr. (Salt Lake City: Deseret Book, 1958).
Trench	Richard Chenevix Trench, *Notes on the Parables of Our Lord,* reprint ed. (Grand Rapids, Michigan: Baker Book House, 1965).

Contents

Introduction

Parables as a teaching tool were not unique to the Lord, but were uniquely used and applied by him to proclaim the kingdom of God. He utilized every facet of daily life in his parables, revealing the depth of his understanding. Crowds thronged to hear him, and through the skillful use of parables he used the simple incidents of life to imprint vividly on their minds his great spiritual truths.

The Gospels of Matthew, Mark, and Luke record the parables randomly. These three Gospels are commonly called the synoptic Gospels, meaning that these writers used a similar approach in presenting the events of Jesus' life. (John often reported events unrecorded in the other Gospels, and he wrote in a different style.) Throughout this book there are frequent references to these three Gospels as the Synoptics, or the synoptic Gospels.

It can be assumed that Jesus gave many parables during his ministry. Mark declares that Jesus taught only in parables to the multitudes: "With many such parables spake he the word unto them . . . but without a parable spake he not unto them" (Mark 4:33–34). Although Mark emphasized this teaching method in the everyday ministry of Jesus, he personally recorded but four of the parables.

Assuming (as we must from Mark's record) that Jesus taught extensively by parables, it would seem obvious that the Gospel writers were very selective in those they chose to record. The same procedure was used when recording the Lord's miracles. Many were performed, but a limited number were recorded.[1] It would appear that the synoptic Gospel writers selected for their records those parables they felt would enhance and clarify the teachings of Jesus as portrayed in their various recordings of the Gospel.

Several points should be considered when studying the parables:

First, the allegorical method of interpretation should be rejected.[2] Although some words or phrases in some of the parables hold interpretive meaning, not every word or phrase need do so.

Second, in all probability Jesus used many parables multiple times, which may have produced variations and adaptations to fit the circumstances of the people being taught.

Third, it is not possible to place the parables in historical order, nor is it necessary, for it is the doctrinal teaching in the parables that is important, not their historical order.

Fourth, it is possible, and perhaps probable, that the parables have undergone changes. This may have occurred because the Gospels were recorded long after the ministry of Jesus concluded. Thus the oral tradition or expression of his teachings may have varied somewhat from the original. This may have produced some of the scriptural discrepancies in the parables, but at this late date it would be impossible to determine these potential variations; therefore there is no practical alternative to accepting the recorded word as authentic.[3]

Thirty-two parables are discussed in this book.[4] Matthew recorded sixteen parables, ten of which are exclusive to his Gospel. Mark recorded four parables, one exclusively, and Luke recorded twenty-one parables, fifteen exclusively. John did not record any parables.

Six of the parables were recorded by more than one of the Synoptic writers. When a parable is recorded by more than one author, the most detailed recording is used here as the primary text. The others are inserted as cross-references only.

The standard King James Version of the Bible is used as the scriptural basis for each parable discussed. Each discussion begins with the relevant scriptural text, quoted in its entirety. Note that when a passage of the quoted scriptural text is used in a discussion, no footnote appears (the whole source having been recorded at the beginning of the discussion). The same is true when a cross-reference is quoted. The name assigned each parable is derived from the parable itself, and is easily recognizable. (Some traditional, alternate names may also appear.)

This book is divided into parts and chapters. Chapter 1 considers the topic of parables in general. Chapters 2 through 11 deal with specific parables. Chapter 12 deals with the message of the parables. Each part and chapter title descriptively defines the doctrinal application of the material that portion contains. This doctrinal classification is my own, derived from what I perceive as the doctrinal emphasis of the parables. Keep in mind that any division or classification of a parable may be open to question, for a parable may have multiple applications to daily life in any age, and its truth may leap over any boundary that attempts to circumscribe it. However, even with this limitation in mind my classification is enthusiastically tendered, that it might add to the clarity and truth of our Lord's teachings.

Parables greatly enhanced the Lord's teachings. Under his masterful usage they became a teaching method "so stimulating, so full of interest . . . in its unapproachable beauty and finish, [that it] stands unrivalled in the annals of human speech."[5]

It is hoped that in the materials that follow the reader will find enlightenment and understanding that will bring further honor and glory to the Lord and his work, and particularly to the parables of Jesus the Messiah.

Part One

The Parables in Perspective

Parables 1

The word *parable* comes from the Greek word *parabole,* as translated from the Hebrew *mashal.* In Greek it means to put forth one thing before or beside another. But in the Hebrew, from which it was originally translated, it has a wider significance, exemplified by the balanced metrical form of the poetic books and teachings of the Old Testament.[1] This method of teaching was not new; "the Parable or Mashal was a mode of instruction already familiar to Israel since the days of the Judges, and was in familiar and constant use among the Rabbis."[2] Jewish teachers used the parable as a common and well-understood method of illustration.[3]

What Is a Parable?

Perhaps to best determine the nature and characteristics of a parable we should first differentiate it from the myth, fable, proverb, and allegory—all of which are other methods of symbolistic teaching. This differentiation enhances the ultimate purpose, definition, and description of the parable.

The Myth: Myths are fictitious traditions or stories. They are usually thought of as being without symbolism of spiritual truth.

However, historically this was not so. Myths were devised to account for natural phenomena and the nature of divine beings. They explained the origin of reality. This reality, the end product of the myth, was determined through the deeds and stories of supernatural beings. The myth usually dealt with forms of creation, but at times also described patterns of behavior. It implied a genuine religious experience, and was not used merely as a vehicle of the truth: It was considered to be the truth itself.[4]

The Fable: The fable, in its widest sense, is an imaginative or fictitious story of any description. Construed more narrowly and in the modern sense, it would be a narrative in prose or verse conveying a moral or useful lesson, but its purpose is generally to entertain or amuse rather than to teach the listener. The characters used in fables are most often animals, but inanimate objects, human beings, or gods (real or mythological) may also appear. Commonly, the fable depicts only a fantasy. The moral is always stated within the structure of the fable itself.[5]

The Proverb: Proverbs are very short, pithy statements in common use. Generally they are preserved through the spoken language and are representative of the behavior of the people who originally preserved them. They transmit tribal wisdom and rules of conduct, and refer to old customs. They commonly summarize well-known fables such as the "wolf in sheep's clothing," or "don't count your chickens before they hatch." A proverb could possibly be described as a condensed parable, an example of which might be "the blind leading the blind."[6]

The Allegory: The allegory can be described as an extended parable, but it is more detailed. It is complex and can involve many relationships. The allegory is imaginative. It usually is expressed through symbols or images of deeper meaning than the surface reveals. Its subjects are generally natural things used as symbols to refer to man, rather than man himself.[7]

The myth, fable, proverb, and allegory may contain elements, or refer to elements, of the spiritual world, but they also involve other facets of life. The parables taught by Jesus, on the other hand, are concerned only with the doctrines of the kingdom and convey spiritual truths.[8]

As stated in the Introduction, parables were in common use prior to and at the time of Jesus Christ.[9] The Jewish writers before

Christ extolled parables as placing the meaning of the Law within the comprehension of the common man.[10] Since the time of Christ, however, Christianity has assigned the word *parable* to mean only those parables expressed in the New Testament and as recited by the Lord. "Others have uttered parables; but Jesus so far transcends them, that He may justly be called the creator of this mode of instruction."[11]

This distinction is unnecessary. It does not distract from the Lord's parables to admit the existence of earlier ones. Rather, this fact enlarges the meaning of the Lord's parables. This common teaching vehicle pictorially carried the truth of the kingdom of God to Christ's listeners, for it used ordinary life with which the listener was totally familiar, and with skillful comparisons made the homeliest trifles symbols of the highest truths of the kingdom.

The parables of Jesus were not scientifically accurate; nor were their facts included or omitted according to the ignorance or knowledge of the hearers. They drew pictures—pictures of life as it was at his time, adapting it to the needs and purposes of the story. The hues, the characters, and the contrasts of the stories were drawn in with words. As Jesus spoke, the great truths of his kingdom passed before the eyes of his audience. At their simplest, the parables of Jesus depicted the common life of the people; step by step they announced with particular clarity the "good news" of the gospel.

The Master Teacher left nothing unused: As he spoke, his listeners could see the sower in the field scattering his seed upon the various soils; there was the miraculous production achieved from a forgotten seed secretly growing or from the leaven as it raised in the woman's dough. One could envision the treasure disclosed to the passerby, previously hidden from the view of all; also the pearl of the traveling merchant from far-off lands; the shepherd searching for the lost sheep while the flock rested calmly; and the woman diligently cleaning to retrieve the coin lost through negligence. The Savior's audience pictured Pharisees, the publicans, the good Samaritan, and stewardship over others' goods; the fig trees as they grew on the hillside and by the paths; and the great supper, to which every Jew looked forward as the culmination of earthly life and entry into the kingdom of God. They envisioned the wedding ceremonies and the feasts; the beggars by the wayside; the laborers awaiting hire; the common mustard plant; and the draw net seen daily on the lake. Using all of these common, simple things, the Lord taught his sublime lessons.

The uniquely applied, well-known scenes of daily life, portrayed in the parables with such vividness, compelled the listener to apply the story and its meaning to the Lord's person and mission. These teaching tools helped Jesus to declare graphically his new gospel.

The nature and characteristics of a parable now begin to unfold:

First, the parable must bear reference to well-known scenes of daily life or events. The picture painted in words by the parable must be familiar to the contemporary mind. Without this, interpretation and application would be impossible.

Second, the circumstances in the parable must be connected to known spiritual realities. This specifically guides the listener's thoughts toward the spiritual application.

Third, in their vivid portrayals, parables draw specific comparisons between abstract spiritual values and real-life situations, thus avoiding general maxims and focusing attention specifically on heavenly doctrine.

Fourth, they were generally not labored literary productions. Sometimes we forget that Jesus, in all probability, composed his parables spontaneously.

The Old Testament contains some parables. The most famous of these was delivered by Samuel to David (2 Samuel 12:1–7). Another familiar parable is in Isaiah (Isaiah 5:1–7). But more than this, there are interesting examples of *living parables* throughout the Old Testament. These "parables" were individuals who lived parabolic lives, representing things higher than themselves, and acting out, as it were, a parable in the eyes of the chosen people. Such was the case of Abraham casting out Hagar (Genesis 21:1–14; Galatians 4:30), Jonah in the belly of the great fish (Jonah 1:17), and David in his hour of agony (Psalm 22). Further, Jehovah commanded Jeremiah to break the potter's vessel (Jeremiah 19:1–11), and to wear the yoke (Jeremiah 27:2; 28:10). All of these stories exemplified parabolic teachings of the

Lord's great truths, which passed before the eyes of his chosen people incorporated in symbolic individuals.

When Jesus taught, he used the situation of the moment that best portrayed to his listeners his divine calling and his witness of the kingdom of heaven. Each of his parables called for an immediate response and conclusion. Some of his listeners understood and accepted, while others understood and rejected. But to some the knowledge imparted by this form of teaching was as the parable of the seed growing secretly.[12] They may not have initially understood or accepted, and the imagery would lie dormant until they were touched by the Spirit, when all things would be brought forth to their remembrance. Then the meaning of what they had heard would unfold, and they would discover the truths of these simple stories.

Why Did Jesus Teach in Parables?

The Lord teaches people in a manner they are familiar with. He "giveth light unto the understanding; for he speaketh unto men according to their language, unto their understanding" (2 Nephi 31:3). He allowed the Nephites "plainness" of speech, for which Jacob was grateful, for he knew that not all people were taught in this manner.

The Nephites had the record of the Jews up to the time that Lehi left Jerusalem, so they were familiar with Jewish teaching methods. In Jacob's opinion the Jews were a "stiffnecked people" who "despised the words of plainness . . . and sought for things that they could not understand" (Jacob 4:14).

The Jaredites were taught "in plain humility . . . in [their] own language" (Ether 12:39), and Joseph Smith was told that the commandments he had received were given "after the manner of their language, that they might come to understanding" (D&C 1:24).

Paul said that "unto the Jews I became as a Jew, that I might gain the Jews. . . . To the weak became I as weak. . . . I am made all things to all men, that I might by all means save some." (1 Corinthians 9:20–23.)

Jesus taught the Jews in parables, a method they were accustomed to. (See chapter 1.) After his first group of parables (recorded in Matthew in chapter 13), the Apostles seemed both surprised and disturbed, for he had undoubtedly been teaching them in plainness. They knew of the linguistic intricacies used by the Jewish leadership in their parables, and were surprised that Jesus was teaching in a similar format. They came to Jesus after the parable of the sower and asked, "Why speakest thou unto them in parables?" (Matthew 13:10.) Jesus gave the following answer (recorded with varying degrees of completeness in all three of the synoptic Gospels):

> Because it is given unto you to know the mysteries of the kingdom of heaven, but to them it is not given.
>
> For whosoever hath, to him shall be given, and he shall have more abundance: but whosoever hath not, from him shall be taken away even that he hath.
>
> Therefore speak I to them in parables: because they seeing see not; and hearing they hear not, neither do they understand.
>
> And in them is fulfilled the prophecy of Esaias, which saith, By hearing ye shall hear, and shall not understand; and seeing ye shall see, and shall not perceive. (Matthew 13:11–14.)

The Lord refers in this passage to Isaiah 6:9, which states, "And he said, Go, and tell this people, Hear ye indeed, but understand not; and see ye indeed, but perceive not."

The Lord did not continually speak in parables after introducing this method of instruction. (See, for example, John 7, 8, 10.) Clearly the rulers and his hearers generally understood the Messianic claim that Jesus presented before them throughout his ministry; on this the scriptures are replete with examples.[13] Yet even as Jesus taught in the temple during the last week of his life, they came to him (seeking an accusation against him) and asked, "How long dost thou make us to doubt? If thou be the Christ, tell us plainly." (John 10:24.) Jesus answered, "I told you, and ye believed not" (John 10:25). Finally, when he clearly stated, "I am the Son of God" (John 10:36), they accused him of blasphemy.

The very nature of the Lord's parables made them readily understandable, and there are examples verifying that his listeners indeed understood him. Jesus taught the parable of the wicked husbandmen,[14] and Matthew reports that the Jews "perceived that he spake of them" (Matthew 21:45). At the conclusion of the parable of the marriage of the king's son,[15] Matthew again reports that they "took counsel how they might entangle him in his talk" (Matthew 22:15).

The parables took the common, everyday aspects of life and unmistakably associated them with the kingdom of God and its teachings. They proclaimed spiritual truth and awakened in the hearer a consciousness of that truth. Their aim was "to show by an example of human action in natural life, how men should act in the sphere of spiritual life."[16]

Thus the teachings of the parables were generally clear to the Lord's audiences. The problem arose in their application of the parables. A perfect example of this occurs in the Old Testament. The prophet Nathan came before King David and told him a parable:

> There were two men in one city; the one rich, and the other poor.
>
> The rich man had exceeding many flocks and herds:
>
> But the poor man had nothing, save one little ewe lamb, which he had bought and nourished up: and it grew up together with him, and with his children; it did eat of his own meat, and drank of his own cup, and lay in his bosom, and was unto him as a daughter.
>
> And there came a traveller unto the rich man, and he spared to take of his own flock and of his own herd, to dress for the wayfaring man that was come unto him; but took the poor man's lamb, and dressed it for the man that was come to him.
>
> And David's anger was greatly kindled against the man; and he said to Nathan, As the Lord liveth, the man that hath done this thing shall surely die:
>
> And he shall restore the lamb fourfold, because he did this thing, and because he had no pity.
>
> And Nathan said to David, Thou art the man. (2 Samuel 12:1–7.)

It is obvious that Nathan (through the Lord) knew of David's involvement with Bathsheba. The parable was presented so that David might recognize his transgression. He clearly understood the story, but he was hearing with the ears of the transgressor and was unwilling to apply the parable to himself. He rightly judged the man in the parable as a sinner, but the parable applied specifically to David, not some stranger, and Nathan so declared.

So it was with the parables of Jesus. He knew the transgressions and errors of the covenant people, and they knew of the anticipated Messiah. He used his parables to help them recognize their sins, repent, accept him as the Savior, and come into the kingdom of God.

Still, the question remains: Why did the Lord teach in parables, and why, when the Apostles questioned Jesus about this teaching method, was his explanation given to them in such a manner? How, by teaching in parables, did Jesus fulfill the prophecy of Isaiah? (See Isaiah 6:9.) In answering these questions let us consider the following: first, the intent of Isaiah's prophecy; and second, the spiritual condition of the people at Jesus' time.

First: The scripture of Isaiah is Messianic.[17] The fact that Jesus applied this scripture to himself is ample evidence of this. But in addition, John attests to its Messianic fulfillment with regard to Christ's miracles (John 12:39–41), and Paul's testimony, both to the Jews (Acts 28:25–27) and to the Romans (Romans 11:7–8), also attests that it was Messianic. Therefore, the rejection of the light taught in the parables (as well as in other teachings) was an open rejection of the prophesied Messiah. To interpret Isaiah otherwise would distort the prophesied Messianic expectation. Jesus did not teach because he wanted to fulfill the prophecies; rather, the prophecies were fulfilled by his teaching.

Second: Israel's spiritual condition at the time of Jesus was one of darkness and apostasy. Since the parables demanded a spiritual response from the hearer, this seems to provide the key to understanding the answer that Jesus gave to his disciples. Jesus declared, "If any man have ears to hear, let him hear" (Mark 4:23). He was inviting his listeners to accept his teachings and apply them in their lives. But he also warned, "Take heed what ye hear. . . . For he that hath, to him shall be given: and he that hath not, from him shall be taken even that which he hath." (Mark 4:24–25.)

The responsibility of those who heard the parables was twofold: first, to recognize Jesus as the Messiah; and second, to learn the doctrines of the kingdom. To hear carelessly or to reject what they heard would draw down the punishments of God upon them. Thus, if the listener was willful, stolid, or indifferent, that attitude would be compounded.[18] The parables conveyed to the hearer religious truths, but his application of those truths was exactly in proportion to his faith and intelligence in spiritual matters (as it was with David in Nathan's parable). To the dull and unintelligent in spiritual matters, the parable was understood only as a story. Seeing, they saw not; hearing, they heard not. To those willing to receive the testimony of Jesus, the parable opened the way to a revelation of the mysteries of God's kingdom.

Those who refused to heed the call fulfilled Isaiah's prophecy of the Messiah. They were the wicked and the unrepentant who would not hear by the Spirit of the Lord, and the parables became a mystery unto them. "Two men may hear the same words; one of them listens in indolence and indifference, the other with active mind intent on learning all that the words can possibly convey; and, having heard, the diligent man goes straightway to do the things commended to him, while the careless one neglects and forgets. The one is wise, the other foolish; one has heard to his eternal profit, the other to his everlasting condemnation."[19]

Therefore, the effect of the parables upon the hearer lay not within the parabolic method of teaching but in the state of spiritual sensibility or insensibility with which the hearer applied it. Although the parables conveyed spiritual instruction to those who accepted Christ, they only served to further darken and dull the spiritually insensible mind.[20] The parables clearly separated the Lord's listeners. To him who had, He would give more. To him who had not, that which he had would be taken away. Parabolic teaching required the listener to recognize his sins and spiritually discern the parables' truths. Then he had to apply those truths in his life.

Now the Lord's reply to the Apostles takes on new meaning. He taught the people in parables (a teaching method they were familiar with) to assist their understanding. If they refused to accept the doctrine so clearly taught, recognize their sins and errors, and repent of them, the parable would become a mystery to them, having no effect on their minds and hearts. If they accepted the doctrine, their minds would be expanded and they would grow spiritually. The Apostles, and others who knew of the doctrine and accepted the Messiah, undoubtedly received instruction from Jesus in "plainness," thus learning the mysteries of God's kingdom. They received light upon light, while those who rejected him and his parables grew darker and darker, until finally the light was gone and they could neither hear, see, nor understand—thus fulfilling the words of Isaiah, for although they saw, yet they "perceived not."

"The appeal [of the Lord] and its success caused scandal. Could this be the coming of the Kingdom of God, when all the moral safeguards laboriously built up by the teachers of the law were cast aside, and the lawless were welcomed into fellowship? To those who raised such objections Jesus appealed in parables with an ironical point. If invited guests did not come to the feast, something must be done to fill the vacant seats."[21]

Classification of Parables

A basic understanding of how the Synoptic writers treated the life of Jesus is enlightening and helpful when discussing the classification of the parables. Even with a cursory reading of the Gospels, it is obvious that the writers did not attempt a complete biography of Christ.[22] The story of the Lord's birth is given in some detail, yet in reality only limited facts are recorded. From his birth and the flight to and from Egypt, no record is given of his childhood other than his experience of teaching in the temple at age twelve (Luke 2:42–49). The next eighteen years are not detailed at all, except for a solitary scripture: "And Jesus increased in wisdom and stature, and in favour with God and man" (Luke 2:52). Thereafter, his three-year ministry is reported with less than the barest detail, except for isolated incidents selected by each Gospel writer. It can therefore be concluded that the intent of the Gospel writers was not to disclose a history of the life of Jesus. Indeed, from "their point of view, [this] would have been almost blasphemy."[23] Rather than appealing to the human-interest aspects of Christ's life, they wrote of the long-awaited Messiah and the advent of the kingdom of God.

Historically, it is generally accepted that the Gospels were directed at specific groups of people. Because Matthew and Luke record all of the parables (except one that is exclusive to Mark), the belief in the historical direction of their works has greatly influenced the classification of their parables. For instance, it is felt that Matthew wrote primarily to Jewish readers, to convince them that Jesus was the expected Messiah. However, Luke apparently wrote to the Gentiles, declaring that Jesus was not just the King of the Jews, but the Savior of the world.[24]

The difficulty with this historical method of examination is obvious. No exact historical order to the parables or the Gospels is possible. In fact, the order in which the parables were recorded may or may not reflect the order in which Jesus gave them. Because so little detail is given of the life of Jesus (except in a few specific instances), only incomplete conclusions can be drawn from the order of the parables in the historical record, and it lends little to the interpretation of the parables to attempt to so order them.

In the final analysis, I feel that it is the doctrinal purpose of the parables that dictates how they are to be classified, and that is the method used in this work. Any classification of the parables may prove limiting, for they have such universality of application to all people, in all times, that they transcend any boundary applied to them. But an examination of the circumstances in which they were given (where possible), and the associated teachings of the kingdom given by the Lord (or revealed elsewhere in the scriptures), leads logically to the classifications I have suggested.

The parables of Jesus were teaching tools. Just as the miracles of Jesus were selected by the writers to exemplify some specific purpose or teaching,[25] so, too, the Synoptic writers selected specific parables to emphasize and clarify Jesus' teachings during his ministry on the earth.

Interpreting Parables

The interpretation of the parables has probably been more troublesome during the centuries since Jesus lived than it was to those who listened to them originally. The following general concepts have been used in this book when interpreting the parables:

First, their interpretation should not be dictated by current or modern needs. No doubt the Lord's parables may be applied to circumstances of any age, and have significance far beyond their original meaning, but we should not force on the original audiences the mores of our age.

Second, and perhaps most important, I have attempted to recover the meaning of the parables as they were originally presented. Jesus taught parables in specific situations, to specific groups of people, and in specific discourses. Therefore, not only the phrases or elements of the parables need to be interpreted and applied, but the experiences described in them must be viewed in the context they were given, not allegorically.[26]

Third, each parable explained or illustrated a principle of the gospel and a teaching of the kingdom of God. Therefore, its interpretation must be in agreement with and couched within all the teachings of the Lord.

Fourth, although the historical placement of the parables by the Gospel writers may give enlightenment and credibility to their interpretation, it is not the principal guideline.

Fifth, the interpretation of the parables must be rationally applied. Any figure of speech is of service only if it is not "carried beyond the bounds of reasonable intent." If it is, it "may become meaningless or even absurd."[27]

With these general concepts of interpretation firmly in mind, I suggest the following:

1. Accept the stories in the parables as examples of real life, and form the interpretation of the parables based on those circumstances. Interpretation should be applied as much as possible to the actual setting contemplated in the Gospels and to those who existed in that setting.

2. Remember, the Lord's parables were delivered to teach and emphasize specific spiritual principles, even though they may be expanded to incorporate general principles.

3. Do not force a meaning on any specific parable, or situation within a parable. Always subordinate the incidents of the parable to the principle for which it was delivered.

4. Do not necessarily regard as parallel parables that are connected by similar imagery.

5. Keep in mind that the illustration used in a particular parable does not always have the same significance elsewhere. For example, in various scriptures leaven signifies the principles of both good and evil. (See Matthew 13:33; 16:6.)

6. The comparisons in the parables may not be complete. The intention appears to have been to draw a picture of life and quickly compare it with heavenly principles.

7. Maintain a proper balance between the various elements of the parable, thus determining the essential elements and disregarding others.

8. Seek the meaning of the parables within the doctrine of the kingdom as taught by Jesus.

Again we note that parables may have significance far beyond their original setting and they may be applied to many situations. But each application should be guided by the particular events which were presented by the Savior, and the way those events apply to the kingdom of God.

Due to the limited record of the Gospel writers not every parable will comply with each of the foregoing requirements. However, each of the parables is "like fruit, which however lovely to look upon, is yet more delectable in its inner sweetness."[28]

Part Two

Teaching the Gospel

The Gospel's Inherent Strength 2

The word *gospel* means "good news," and Jesus offered it first to the Jews. It was his declaration that he was the long-awaited Messiah and had come to establish his kingdom.

He taught the laws and doctrines of the kingdom in many ways, but with a single purpose—to save the souls of men. Jesus dedicated his life to this purpose. He taught openly and in private, to multitudes and to individuals. He used discourses to explain his principles, miracles to witness them, and parables to add clarity and richness to his teachings and strength to his testimony.

The Sower

Matthew 13:3—9, 18—23

3. And he spake many things unto them in parables, saying, Behold, a sower went forth to sow;

4. And when he sowed, some seeds fell by the way side, and the fowls came and devoured them up:

5. Some fell upon stony places, where they had not much earth: and forthwith they sprung up, because

they had no deepness of
earth:
6. And when the sun
was up, they were scorched;
and because they had no
root, they withered away.
7. And some fell among
thorns; and the thorns
sprung up, and choked
them:
8. But other fell into
good ground, and brought
forth fruit, some an hundredfold, some sixtyfold,
some thirtyfold.
9. Who hath ears to
hear, let him hear.
18. Hear ye therefore the
parable of the sower.
19. When any one heareth the word of the kingdom, and understandeth it
not, then cometh the wicked
one, and catcheth away that
which was sown in his
heart. This is he which
received seed by the way
side.
20. But he that received
the seed into stony places,
the same is he that heareth
the word, and anon with joy
receiveth it;
21. Yet hath he not root
in himself, but dureth for a
while: for when tribulation
or persecution ariseth because of the word, by and
by he is offended.
22. He also that received
seed among the thorns is he
that heareth the word; and
the care of this world, and
the deceitfulness of riches,
choke the word, and he becometh unfruitful.
23. But he that received
seed into the good ground is
he that heareth the word,
and understandeth it; which
also beareth fruit, and bringeth forth, some an hundredfold, some sixty, some
thirty.

Cross-references

Mark 4:3–9, 14–20 Luke 8:5–8, 11–15

The parable of the sower is recorded in all three Synoptics, but Matthew is used here as the primary text. Matthew records six additional parables in the same chapter as the sower,[1] Mark records three others (one differing from Matthew), and Luke only records the sower. All of the Synoptics note the parable of the sower as the beginning of the parabolic style of teaching by Jesus.

By this time the Lord's ministry had reached great heights, and his fame brought multitudes to hear him (Matthew 13:2; Mark 4:1). But his plain and straightforward teaching had produced some bitter hostility (Mark 3:6), and "many of his disciples went back, and walked no more with him" (John 6:66). His success, however, inspired the cunning Jewish leadership to concoct the Beelzebub argument in an effort to confuse the people.[2]

But on the day he gave the parable of the sower, the magnitude of the Lord's presence drew people from "every city," and as he was wont to do on other occasions, he separated himself from the multitude, boarded a ship, and pushed a little way from shore, that he might teach the multitude as they stood on the shoreline.

With the beautiful Sea of Galilee behind him and the fruitful fields of the countryside before him, he taught the multitude the parable of the sower. Although all those listening to the Lord yearned for the Messiah's presence, the parable depicted to them the awful reality of the reception they and all mankind would give Him and His gospel. It reflected that reception both historically (that which had already occurred in the ministry of Jesus) and futuristically (that which would yet occur as the gospel was taken to all the world). It not only portrayed Jesus as the Sower, but indicated that all others who delivered his message of salvation would also be thought of as sowers.

The scenes the Lord described were very familiar to his audience. They had seen the circumstances time and time again. This was real life—a situation that could not be misunderstood. As the parable unfolded, the audience could envision the sower walking up and down his field spreading the seed by hand. Or perhaps they could see the seed in bags strapped on the sides of an animal, as was also the custom. Small holes had been punctured in the bottom of the bags; from these the seeds would randomly fall as the animal was led or driven up and down the field.[3]

The seed represented the word of God—the gospel. It was sown by the sower indiscriminately. There was no limit to its quantity, and it fell on all of the ground, that all might be given equal opportunity to bring forth fruit.

This was the scene presented to the mind of the hearer as the Master told his story, but these were not the important elements of the parable. Neither the sower nor the seed emphasized the eternal principles being taught by the Master.[4] These eternal principles were being taught in the description of the soil on which the seed fell. This was the main thrust of the parable. The soil represented the hearts of men.

First: The soil found by the "wayside." This was the most hardened of the soils. As the story unfolded, the audience could envision the hardened path or road through the fields that had been continually trampled by the feet of travelers. They might have turned to see the fields that spread out behind them, and the hardened paths or roads that they had walked on in order to hear the Master.

As the sower spread the seed, some fell on this wayside soil. Unable to penetrate the hardness of the surface, the seed lay upon the ground and was easily destroyed by the birds that came and devoured it. Some of mankind could be compared to this wayside soil, perhaps some in the very audience that stood before the Lord. Their hearts were so worn down and bereft of the Spirit by constant sin that they would not receive his word. They had no comprehension or understanding of the teachings of the Messiah. All that Jesus spoke was meaningless to them, and the spiritual significance of his words was totally deadened by their worldly thoughts, actions, and total opposition to the word of God. These were "men who have no principle of righteousness in themselves, and whose hearts are full of iniquity, and have no desire for the principles of truth, [and] do not understand the word of truth when they hear it. The devil taketh away the word of truth out of their hearts, because there is no desire for righteousness in them."[5]

These were the men and women of Christ's day (and of future days) who totally rejected him. They would accept neither his teachings nor his miracles. Their hearts were so perverted by sin and by opposition to the Messiah that there was no possibility of change in them. Their lack of understanding and unwillingness to apply his teachings in their lives made it possible for the wicked one to "[catch] away that which was sown in [their hearts]," because "there is no desire for righteousness in them." Because of the hardness of their hearts, they rejected the gospel in its entirety and did not allow the seed to commence growth.

Second: The soil described as "stony places." This is not to be interpreted as soil mingled with stones, but rather a thin layer of soil covering a rocky surface that is deceitfully hidden beneath, out of the sight of men.[6] This soil described the majority of the people who followed Jesus—the multitudes of curiosity seekers (Luke 14:25–33). This soil caught the seeds, and the seeds quickly sprang up. The people represented by this soil heard the word with gladness and enjoyed the sweetness of each discourse, but they had no root. These were they with temporary faith, who ultimately gave their earthly life more importance than the riches of the Lord's kingdom.[7] They did not stubbornly reject the word, nor did they overtly conspire to destroy Jesus. They merely lacked the roots of commitment, and their faith quickly withered and died.[8] Of these the Lord said, "Yet hath he not root in himself, but dureth for a while." These were the people offended by the word during persecution or tribulation. The Lord described these souls in the Sermon on the Mount as they who had built upon the sand, and when "the rain descended, and the floods came, and the winds blew, and beat upon that house," it fell (Matthew 7:27).

The soil found in stony places, like the soil by the wayside, described those who rejected the Messiah. Because of their sins and their desire for the praise of men, their hearts were set against him. The gospel meant less to them than the way they were living; therefore they would not change. They would not take up his cross—they would not repent—they would not believe. They could not understand the parable because they refused, in their disbelief and rejection of Christ, to apply the parable to themselves.

The Lord next described the soils where the seed had a chance to grow:

Third: The soil "full of thorns" when the seed was sown. Here there was no lack of good soil, as was the case in the first two examples, but this soil was encumbered with weeds that would prevent the seed from growing.

The Old Testament provides an analogy that brings understanding to the interpretation of the seed growing in this type of soil. After God created the earth, he created man and placed him in the Garden of Eden, wherein all things grew naturally. Adam was commanded not to partake of the forbidden fruit, and was told that he would be punished for disobedience. Adam partook of the fruit and in so doing, transgressed, and was brought before God to receive the results of his transgression. God expelled him from the Garden of Eden, and cursed the earth for his sake, stating, "Thorns also and thistles shall it bring forth to thee; and thou shalt eat the herb of the field; in the sweat of thy face shalt thou eat bread, till thou return unto the ground" (Genesis 3:17—19). Adam could no longer draw upon the natural growth of the earth for his food, for there would be thorns growing in its soil. But by his labor, or the sweat of his brow, he could toil and properly prepare the soil so that it might produce the food that he needed.

So likewise was the third soil portrayed in the parable of the sower. It would not produce because of the careless husbandman. Because he did not remove the weeds, thorns, and thistles from the ground, the Lord said of him, "the care of this world, and the deceitfulness of riches, choke the word, and he [the husbandman] becometh unfruitful." The husbandman professed spiritual life, but there was no power to his conviction. The cares of the world were more important to him than the word of God.[9] Jesus cautioned his Apostles that they must ever "take heed to [themselves]" that their hearts be not "overcharged with surfeiting, and drunkenness, and cares of this life" (Luke 21:34). They could not serve two masters (Matthew 6:24).

Fourth: The soil described as "good ground." It is only here that fruitful growth occurs. Those exemplified by this type of soil hear the word and understand it. Although they may sin (as do all men) they recognize their sins, and without self-justification that would alter the truth, they repent of their transgressions. These have prepared their hearts to receive the word of God as represented by the seed.

An example of this type of individual is given in the New Testament in the story of Zacchaeus. He was accounted by the Pharisees and rulers of the Jews as a sinner because of his occupation—he was a tax collector. When the Lord met Zacchaeus he asked if he could dine at his home, and Zacchaeus graciously received the Lord into his house. There he told Jesus of his personal spiritual preparation. He had given to the poor one-half of his goods, and he declared that if he perchance took from any man by false accusation, he restored it to him fourfold. In this confession Jesus saw the true believer and declared, "This day is salvation come to this house" (Luke 19:1–9).

Another example that is even more cogent is that of Nathanael when he was called to follow Jesus. As Nathanael approached Jesus (never having seen the Lord before), Jesus said, "Behold an Israelite indeed, in whom is no guile!" (John 1:47.) Nathanael acknowledged the salutation of the Lord, for he had properly prepared himself to receive the word. He had been totally faithful to the light that he had, and was prepared to receive more when it came.

These are the four soils of the parable depicted by the Master. It was into these soils that the seed was scattered. The condition of the soil represented the condition of the heart of the hearer and the preparation he had made in his spiritual quest. Some hearts were so hard that they would not receive the gospel at all; others rejected it because of their lack of preparation to receive the word. Only the last group, representing one-fourth of the people (if the parable were to be taken literally), had prepared themselves sufficiently that when they received of the word it brought forth good fruit.

The description of the soils and the interpretation thereof was the main purpose of this parable. However, it seems to have a secondary purpose, found in the declaration by the Lord of the fruits brought forth from the good soil.[10] Even here there was a difference in the quantity of fruit brought forth. It was at that certain moment of harvest (or the judgment) when the field had to be ready, but not all the "good soil" produced the same amount of fruit—there was a variable harvest.

The seeds had been sown at the same time and had the same amount of time to grow. Only the soils were different. The seed was abundant and spread on all the soils equally. Each received the same rain, light, and heat, but even the good soil produced varying results, for as the parable pointed out, it produced some an hundredfold, some sixty, and some thirty. Although those represented by the good soil had prepared themselves sufficiently to receive of the seed and to produce fruit, they still struggled with the successful use of the seed itself.[11]

Various applications of this parable can be made to the gospel in everyday life, but the simplicity of the parable and its common scenery were contemporary with the time, place, and circumstance in which Jesus was laboring, and depicted the reaction of the people to him and his ministry. The sower performed his job in a typical and recognizable manner, and the seed was good. Only the soils were different. The parable taught clearly where the responsibility lay with regard to the kingdom of God and the reception of the gospel. It was not with the sower and it was not in the seed—it was in the "soil," the heart of man.

The Wheat and Tares

Matthew 13:24–30, 37–43

24. Another parable put he forth unto them, saying, The kingdom of heaven is likened unto a man which sowed good seed in his field:

25. But while men slept, his enemy came and sowed tares among the wheat, and went his way.

26. But when the blade was sprung up, and brought forth fruit, then appeared the tares also.

27. So the servants of the householder came and said unto him, Sir, didst not thou sow good seed in thy field? from whence then hath it tares?

28. He said unto them, An enemy hath done this. The servants said unto him, Wilt thou then that we go and gather them up?

29. But he said, Nay; lest while ye gather up the tares, ye root up also the wheat with them.

30. Let both grow together until the harvest: and in the time of harvest I will say to the reapers, Gather ye together first the tares, and bind them in bundles to burn them: but gather the wheat into my barn.

37. He answered and said unto them, He that soweth the good seed is the Son of man;

38. The field is the world; the good seed are the children of the kingdom; but the tares are the children of the wicked one;

39. The enemy that sowed them is the devil; the harvest is the end of the world; and the reapers are the angels.

40. As therefore the tares are gathered and burned in the fire; so shall it be in the end of this world.

41. The Son of man shall

send forth his angels, and they shall gather out of his kingdom all things that offend, and them which do iniquity;

42. And shall cast them into a furnace of fire: there shall be wailing and gnashing of teeth.

43. Then shall the righteous shine forth as the sun in the kingdom of their Father. Who hath ears to hear, let him hear.

This parable is recorded only by Matthew, and is the second of the recorded parables that the Lord interpreted for the Apostles. It is a realistic story garnered from the agricultural life of his day.[12] It is told vividly and naturally, simple in its terms, yet complicated in its interpretation; and it is perhaps the most un-Jewish of the parables.[13]

The first problem in interpreting this parable arises when the Lord opens the parable with a quick analogy, likening the kingdom of heaven to a man who sowed good seed in his field. However, the kingdom of heaven is not actually like the man, the seed, or the field. The Lord used this type of introduction in several of his parables.[14] It is called a datival introduction, and is part of the puzzle to be solved by the hearer. Because the Jews had such a complete misconception of what the kingdom of heaven would be like, Jesus attempted to teach them the truth through examples that would be familiar to them. However, the datival introduction required the hearer to discern the identity of the kingdom of heaven as he progressed through the parabolic story.[15]

The Lord's interpretation to the Apostles verifies that the kingdom of heaven was not like any part of the parable. Therefore, what is it like? In this instance it is like the Church, even though unidentified in the parable itself.[16] The Church is the kingdom of heaven upon the earth, and the parabolic story described what happened therein. This description applies to the Church whenever it is in existence (not just at the time of Christ); therefore, the parable applies specifically to the following:[17]

1. To the meridian of time when Jesus established the Church, to the Church as it flourished thereafter, and to the reasons behind its eventual apostasy.

2. To the establishment of the Church on the Western Hemi-

sphere, which occurred after the resurrection of Jesus and his visit there (3 Nephi). (Again the Church flourished, but eventually was overcome by the evils of the world.)

3. To the restoration of the gospel and the establishment of the Church in the latter days (D&C 86). (Although the Church is flourishing today, evil exists within its membership along with the good. However, in this, the last dispensation, the Church will not again be overcome and taken from the earth (D&C 13). Thus the growth of weak or evil members of the Church, as they exist side by side with those who actively seek righteousness, will continue until the judgment, or the "end of the world."

4. To future light and knowledge to be restored to the Church by the Lord, for the parable prophetically explained that the evil sower of seed will always mimic the Lord's good work in an attempt to destroy His earthly kingdom.

Even though this parable does not directly describe the kingdom of heaven or the Church, it does describe what takes place within it. The simple reference to the seed, the blade, and the fruit (whether good or evil) pertains to and represents the members of the Church, or "the children of the kingdom." The sower of the good seed is the Son of Man, or Jesus Christ. The sower of the bad seed (the enemy) is the devil or Satan. This moral battle between these two great sources of good and evil takes place in the "field" (or the world).

The good and bad seed represents the members of the Church. The wheat sown by the Lord, the Son of Man, is the good seed. The enemy (the devil) mimicked the Lord by oversowing the same field (or the entire Church) with a degenerate kind of wheat (the tares), so that he might easily confuse and deceive the mind of man.

Oversowing was a common deed of enmity in Christ's time, and was a form of malice (with little risk) that resulted in great harm. It was a form of enemy retribution, and would have been very familiar to the hearers of the parable.[18]

The two types of seed grew together and at first were indistinguishable the one from the other. They were watered and cultivated together until the time of harvest, when they brought forth fruit—then the tares were discovered.

An interesting association can be made between this parable and that of the sower. In the sower, three of the four soils were unable to produce fruit at all. Only in the last soil, the good soil, was fruit produced. If we associate the wheat and tares with the good soil (where one-fourth of the seed brought forth fruit), it sheds added light on the difficulty even those in the good soil will have in their struggle to overcome evil and the temptations of the world.

The second problem of interpretation surrounds the man who sowed the good seed. The parable of the wheat and tares applies to the Church whenever it is established upon the earth, so this phrase must be reconciled with the interpretation given by Jesus in his ministry (that he was the Sower) and the interpretation revealed in the latter-day restoration of the gospel identifying the Apostles as the sowers (D&C 86:2).

When he interpreted the parable, Jesus told his disciples, "He that soweth the good seed is the Son of man." This interpretation is obvious, for the Church was first established by Jesus in the meridian of time; therefore, the sower was the Savior himself. But he would not always remain on the earth with the Church. He therefore had to prepare the Apostles to continue the work. To do this, he gave them his authority and charged them to take his gospel to all the world (Matthew 28:19–20). Thereafter, under his authority, they in turn became sowers of the seed.

This same situation existed in the establishment of the Church on the Western Hemisphere. Jesus came personally to establish his Church. He taught both the people in general and his disciples in particular. When his ministry to the Nephites was complete he departed, again bestowing authority on his twelve chosen disciples, and charging them to continue to spread the gospel (3 Nephi 11-28). Thus, they became sowers.

Today, after a long and complete apostasy from the truth, the Lord has again established his Church (Joseph Smith—History 1:17–74). He has called, authorized, and empowered Apostles to spread the gospel throughout the world.[19] The basic organizational structure of the Church has been the same in all ages. The head of the Church is Jesus Christ. During his ministry he lived and walked among the children of men, and he himself began to sow the seed as he established his Church. When he completed his earthly ministry he empowered his Apostles to continue the work. Their authority came directly from him, as did the authority of the disciples on the Western Hemisphere and those of the latter days. Therefore, Jesus could accurately interpret the parable of the wheat and tares to his Apostles, both of his time and in the latter days, and declare that they, as well as he, "were the sowers of the seed" (D&C 86:2).

Next, the parable openly declared that "while men slept, his enemy came and sowed tares among the wheat, and went his way." The enemy was specifically identified by the Lord as the devil, and that fact is confirmed in the latter-day application of the parable found in the Doctrine and Covenants (D&C 86:3). The sowing of the tares within the Church and throughout the world represents the open hostility of Satan toward the Savior.[20] This is the moral battle within the Church between good and the evil initiated by the devil. He is a mimicker of Christ, lying in wait to carefully sow a degenerate gospel, that he might stealthily deceive the children of the Father and lead them carefully down to hell (2 Nephi 28:21–22).[21]

The parable now reaches its conclusion and the third problem of its interpretation. The two seeds grow and the blades spring up to the point where fruit is discernible. It is at this time that the servants of the sower recognize that not all in the field is of the good seed, or of the righteous. They ask the Lord who sowed the tares, and he tells them that the enemy (or the devil) was responsible. Again the servants earnestly ask, "Wilt thou then that we go and gather them up?" The Lord quickly responds, "Nay; lest while ye gather up the tares, ye root up also the wheat with them." It was not the time to harvest the wheat or to disturb the growth of the Church while it was newly established and tender.

The servants (or authorities of the Church) were now confronted with two situations concerning its evil or corrupt members. First, if they stepped forward and plucked the evil growth out, they might cause harm to the good growth. Because the Church was young and inexperienced, the plucking up of the tares would probably disrupt the operation of the Church itself; this, in its infancy, might be a threat to its very existence. The good and evil were therefore allowed to grow and ripen together.

Herein is found an important, secondary lesson of the parable—the teaching of patience, long-suffering, and tolerance within the Church by its authorities.[22] Those who choose evil over good should have sufficient time to either repent of their transgressions or mature in their iniquity, so that at the time of final judgment they can easily be discerned from the righteous.

Second, there is a caution in the Lord's answer concerning man's capability of judging his fellowman (as opposed to the judgment of the Lord). Man may judge his fellowman for purposes of preserving the integrity of the Church and to effectively outline procedural repentance—thus allowing the repentant sinner the opportunity of restoring himself to the Church. But those permanent judgments pertaining to our eternal existence are to be left for a later time (D&C 86:6) and a greater Judge.[23]

Through these instructions, the Church could avoid the error committed by the Jews under the Law of Moses. In their over-zealous effort to preserve and protect the purity of the Law, they had condemned their people as violators of it. Their punctilious eradication of "evil" had destroyed the very Law given to protect them. The leadership of the Lord's Church was cautioned and instructed through this parable so that they might not duplicate this error.

Thus, the parable declared that the wheat and the tares should grow together "until the harvest." Then the Lord will instruct the reapers, "Gather ye together first the tares, and bind them in bundles to burn them: but gather the wheat into my barn." (See also D&C 86:7.) The reapers are the Lord's angels, and they will be sent forth to gather out of his kingdom "all things that offend, and them which do iniquity." The wicked will be cast into the fiery furnace (or representatively destroyed), while the righteous will be gathered into the kingdom of God.[24] This was the reason the wheat and the tares were allowed to grow together, and why the servants were restrained from plucking out the tares when they first appeared. The books of accountability for the children of men are not balanced daily.[25] The wicked are allowed to ripen temporarily, and in the final day, the evil and the good shall stand together face to face—Christ and the anti-Christ—distinguishable in all their deeds: the one totally light and the other in total darkness.

One last note should be made concerning the title "the Son of Man." Although this was the most common appellation the Lord ascribed to himself, the title was not prevalent anywhere else in the scriptures. However, Daniel used the title in his vision pertaining to the Messiah (Daniel 7:13), so the leadership of the Jews would have recognized this title as a claim by Jesus to the Messiahship. Evidence of this recognition is recorded in the reaction of the Jewish rulers to the interrogation of Stephen and his subsequent vision. Stephen preached before the rulers with such power and force that they became enraged. During his ensuing trial the heavens opened and Stephen said, "Behold, I see the heavens opened, and the Son of man standing on the right hand of God." This declaration was more than the Jewish leadership could stand, and in their rage they "stopped their ears, and ran upon him with one accord." He was cast out of the city and stoned to death (Acts 7:54–58).

The Mustard Seed, The Leaven, The Seed Growing Secretly

After hearing the parables of the sower and the wheat and tares, the disciples undoubtedly experienced some despair, for the sower limited the fertility of the gospel (the seed) to only one-fourth of the ground, and because of the tares, even that ground contained great obstacles that could destroy the production of the fruit and thus dampen the enthusiasm of the harvest. Therefore, the Lord gave three more short parables on this subject to help the disciples see that the power of the kingdom was far beyond that created by men, or that mimicked by the devil.

These three parables—the mustard seed, the leaven, and the seed growing secretly—further illustrate the disparity of belief previously discussed in connection with the sower and the wheat and tares. The perception held by the children of Israel concerning the anticipated Messiah was incorrect. The Jews expected the kingdom of God to come in great political strength that would relieve them of the bondage that had been inflicted upon them for hundreds of years.[26] In this context these parables were very un-Jewish, since they showed that the kingdom of God would not come in the manner the Jews anticipated. This further separated the true followers of Christ from those who merely professed belief.

Their anticipated Messiah was not like Jesus. Jesus grew up in a despised province. Even from one who would be his disciple came the disdainful question, "Can there any good thing come out of Nazareth?" (John 1:46.) The Jewish leadership said, "Shall Christ come out of Galilee?" (John 7:41), and "Search, and look: for out of Galilee ariseth no prophet" (John 7:52).

The Savior entered his public ministry at the age of thirty, and taught for only three years in Jerusalem and its neighboring villages. His knowledge of the Law was unsurpassed, but the tradition-bound populace wondered, "How knoweth this man letters, having never learned?" (John 7:15.) His converts were not generally of the leadership or the learned, but were of the poor, the sinners, the Gentiles, and the uneducated. And at the conclusion of his ministry, he fell into the hands of his enemies and died a shameful death on the cross.

Although this was not the Messiah or kingdom the Jews traditionally expected, such was the commencement of the kingdom of God, and it was clearly illustrated in the parables of the mustard seed, the leaven, and the seed growing secretly.

Before discussing these parables, it might be helpful to note their similarities:

First: The use of the seed as a simile to describe the planting or growth of the gospel was a common one. It was used by the Lord many times, and had been used by the rabbis before him.[27]

Second: These parables have what was previously defined as a datival introduction, wherein the Lord declares that the kingdom is like unto something, whereas the kingdom may or may not be like the initial analogy or any portion of the parable.[28]

Third: These parables contain three elements that pertain to the kingdom of God.

1. The seed (or leaven);
2. The capacity of the seed for growth;
3. The harvest, or the great results of the reaping of the fruit.

All of these items are supplementary and complementary to the parables of the sower and the wheat and tares.

The following paragraphs illustrate the common points of interpretation in all of these parables:

1. *The seed or leaven.* In each of the parables, the seed (or leaven) represents the small beginnings of the kingdom of God (or his church) on the earth. All the people that come to the earth will have the opportunity to accept the Lord and come into his kingdom. In the mustard seed and the leaven, this principle is applied openly. In the seed growing secretly, the application is hidden and the growth of the seed is not immediately anticipated.

2. *The capacity of the seed.* This shows the power and influence of the gospel, whether from without, as in the mustard seed, or from within, as in the leaven. It demonstrates how the secret capabilities of the seed can act upon those who might initially ignore the gospel, yet later receive it, as in the seed growing secretly. In all three parables the seed is sustained by its own power. Paul accurately described this method of growth in the kingdom of God when he said, "I have planted, Apollos watered; but God gave the increase" (1 Corinthians 3:6).

3. *The sower of the seed.* Whether the sowing of the seed was done by the Son of God or his agents is immaterial, for it could be interpreted as both. Regardless of who applies, nourishes, or strengthens the seed, it is only the power of the seed itself, as drawn upon by the Spirit of the Holy Ghost, that gives the increase and produces the fruit.

4. *The harvest.* The final stages of the parables teach that the gospel will not be destroyed from within or without, nor will the devil succeed against it.

Through these parables, the Lord gave the disciples great hope that the kingdom of God would prevail and give to all men the protection they needed to return to the Father.

These three short parables, as well as those of the sower and the wheat and tares, apply directly to the kingdom of God as established by the Savior, but their simplicity and beauty can stretch forward and encompass the restoration of the gospel in the latter days. The sower and the wheat and tares deal with the *tribulation* of accepting the truth. The mustard seed, the leaven, and the seed growing secretly teach the *joy* of accepting the truth. These parables assured the Apostles of the kingdom's eventual success. From small beginnings, the gospel would grow to encompass the whole earth.

The Mustard Seed

Mark 4:30–32

30. And he said, Whereunto shall we liken the kingdom of God? or with what comparison shall we compare it?
31. It is like a grain of mustard seed, which, when it is sown in the earth, is less than all the seeds that be in the earth:
32. But when it is sown, it groweth up, and becometh greater than all herbs, and shooteth out great branches; so that the fowls of the air may lodge under the shadow of it.

Cross-references

Matthew 13:31–32 Luke 13:18–19

The parable of the mustard seed was an exciting little story that described what the kingdom of God would eventually be like. It was in such contrast to the Jewish expectation that it was a difficult parable for them to understand, but the implication of the parable could not have gone unnoticed.[29] They expected the Messianic kingdom to be great, both at its inception and at its conclusion. But the gospel Jesus offered was not initially impressive, and the Jews could not envision it providing for their temporal and spiritual salvation. They ritualistically observed the Law of Moses with its complicated doctrines and interpretations, and their view of acceptance before God required years of study and application of the Law before an individual could qualify for the kingdom. But Jesus readily offered the gospel to all who would come unto him: the weak, the sinner, and the unlearned as well as the learned.

The mustard seed was used as an example because of the smallness of the seed as compared to the size of its product. It was not a tree, but a giant shrub; yet the shrub produced shade for those who passed by, and provided a lodging for birds that offered protection from the elements. This type of comparison had been used by Old Testament prophets and would have been familiar to the hearers (see Ezekiel 17:23; 31:6; Daniel 4:10—22).

The immense growth inherent in the mustard seed described the destiny of the kingdom of God, and undoubtedly gave the disciples great hope. They could see that the kingdom would eventually grow far beyond the limited size evidenced thus far in the ministry of Christ and the growth which they themselves would produce in their own ministry after the Lord's resurrection. Their work was only the beginning. The seed (or gospel) would sprout forth quickly under their efforts, but would eventually be trodden down by the apostasy foreshadowed in the parable of the wheat and tares. Only in the restoration of the gospel in the latter days would the parable of the mustard seed attain its fulfillment.[30]

The refuge provided by the branches of the tree represented the protection the gospel gives those who will embrace its requirements. As Elder James E. Talmage stated, "So the seed of truth is vital, living, and capable of such development as to furnish spiritual food and shelter to all who come seeking."[31]

In the application of the parable to the restoration of the gospel in modern times, Joseph Smith specifically declared:

> Now we can discover plainly that this figure is given to represent the Church as it shall come forth in the last days. Behold, the Kingdom of Heaven is likened unto it. Now, what is like unto it?
>
> Let us take the Book of Mormon, which a man took and hid in his field, securing it by his faith, to spring up in the last days, or in due time; let us behold it coming forth out of the ground, which is indeed accounted the least of all seeds, but behold it branching forth, yea, even towering, with lofty branches, and God-like majesty, until it, like the mustard seed, becomes the greatest of all herbs. . . . Behold, then is not this the Kingdom of Heaven that is raising its head in the last days in the majesty of its God, even the Church of the Latter-day Saints, like an impenetrable, immovable rock in the midst of the mighty deep, exposed to the storms and tempests of Satan, but has, thus far, remained steadfast.[32]

The Leaven

Luke 13:20–21

20. And again he said, Whereunto shall I liken the kingdom of God?
21. It is like leaven, which a woman took and hid in three measures of meal, till the whole was leavened.

Cross-reference

Matthew 13:33

This small parable is most un-Jewish, and to the unbelievers, most mysterious.[33] It is very similar to the mustard seed, as both the mustard seed and the leaven symbolically possess the inherent vitality necessary for the development of the kingdom of God.[34]

The Lord used leaven in this parable as the symbol of the kingdom of God, although at other times he used it to describe evil influences infecting the kingdom (Mark 8:15). Here, however, the wholesome influence of the leaven permeates dead Judaism with the vitality of the kingdom's truth. Unlike the outward growth of the mustard seed, the leaven grew from within, indicating that when heard, the gospel could pervade and transform a person's whole life.[35] The parable emphasizes the end results of the leaven rather than its rapid growth, and therefore adds to the thought initially taught in the mustard seed.

The establishment of the gospel by the Savior did not reach its ultimate destiny (of permeating the entire earth) during Christ's lifetime, nor during the lifetime of his Apostles, and the fulfillment of the parable would not come until after the restoration of the gospel. Therefore, the parable prophesied of the final triumph of the kingdom of God in the latter days. When Joseph Smith was questioned about the parable he responded, "It alluded expressly to the last days, when there should be but little faith on the earth, and it should leaven the whole world; also there shall be safety in Zion and Jerusalem, and in the remnants whom the Lord our God shall call."[36] In another setting the Prophet Joseph said, "It may be understood that the Church of the Latter-day Saints has taken its rise from a little leaven that was put into three witnesses. Behold, how much this is like the parable! It is fast leavening the lump, and will soon leaven the whole."[37]

And so this little parable, so mysterious to the Jews of Christ's day, and seemingly so simple in its application, had a far-reaching impact that would not see its final fulfillment until the angels should receive permission to go forth and separate the wheat from the tares and gather the good fruit into the kingdom.

The Seed Growing Secretly

Mark 4:26–29

26. And he said, So is the kingdom of God, as if a man should cast seed into the ground;

27. And should sleep, and rise night and day, and the seed should spring and grow up, he knoweth not how.

28. For the earth bringeth forth fruit of herself; first the blade, then the ear, after that the full corn in the ear.

29. But when the fruit is brought forth, immediately he putteth in the sickle, because the harvest is come.

Finally, we come to the seed growing secretly, the only parable that is exclusively recorded by Mark. This parable elaborates on the inherent strength of the gospel as discussed in the mustard seed and the leaven, but adds the dimension of time between hearing the gospel and accepting it.

After the seed is sown its growth commences, "dependent on the law inherent in seed and soil," but even more dependent "on Heaven's blessing of sunshine and showers, till the moment of ripeness, when the harvest-time is come."[38]

The parable describes the vitality of the gospel in the listener even though the listener does not immediately accept it.[39] The constant growth of the seed is assured and the harvest is anticipated (Revelation 14:14–15).

The Lord used these three parables to give his Apostles encouragement after he had described the difficulties the kingdom would encounter in the parables of the sower and the wheat and tares. Peter gave the same type of encouragement to the Saints when he spoke of "Being born again, not of corruptible seed, but of incorruptible, by the word of God, which liveth and abideth for ever. For all flesh is as grass, and all the glory of man as the flower of grass. The grass withereth, and the flower thereof falleth away: But the word of the Lord endureth for ever. And this is the word which by the gospel is preached unto you." (1 Peter 1:23–25.)

There will always be obstacles in the path of those who receive the kingdom, but if the path is followed, the harvest is assured.

The Gospel Once Discovered 3

Throughout his entire ministry, Jesus preached the nearness of the kingdom of God and laid claim to the Messiahship. The coming of the Messiah was looked for in all that was done in Jewish life. The Old Testament prophesied of it and the Law that governed the lives of the children of Israel prepared them for that great event. But their perception of what the Messiah would be like was incorrect. They anticipated that the Messiah would establish a political kingdom, not a spiritual one. The gospel Jesus preached was intended to save souls eternally, not the nation temporally.

It was this choice, between spiritual salvation and temporal existence, that faced the people Jesus taught. They had to decide for themselves just how important the gospel was. Jesus clearly taught the course that would lead to eternal life. Some believed on him and some did not.

A Candle Under a Bushel

Matthew 5:14–15

14. Ye are the light of the world. A city that is set on an hill cannot be hid.
15. Neither do men light a candle, and put it under a bushel, but on a candlestick; and it giveth light unto all that are in the house.

Cross-references

Mark 4:21–22 Luke 8:16–17

Most writers do not refer to these few sentences as a parable, but this little analogy, couched in the general parabolic form, is an excellent introduction to the parables that describe what is required of those who have discovered the gospel. The saying is a simple one and is obvious in its interpretation. One does not light a lamp or turn on a light in order to hide it so that no one will see it. This analogy was given so that those who heard the gospel would fully understand their responsibility pertaining to it. It was not to be something that they were ashamed of, nor was it to be neglected, but it was to be received with gladness and expanded upon.

Some of the Jews who heard the gospel were reluctant to associate with it openly. The best example of this might be Nicodemus. He first went to Jesus by night to ask questions that he might better understand His teachings (John 3:1–5). Later, he timidly defended Jesus before the Sanhedrin (John 7:50–51), and at the burial of Jesus, he provided certain ointments to adorn the Lord's body (John 19:39). We do not know whether he became an open follower of the Lord.

The leaders and many of the people who initially accepted Jesus were very reluctant to openly acknowledge him. They hid the light rather than acknowledge and proclaim it.

This teaching, parabolic in form, supplements the parables that were given to symbolize the importance of the gospel once discovered.

The Hidden Treasure

Matthew 13:44

44. Again, the kingdom of heaven is like unto treasure hid in a field; the which when a man hath found, he hideth, and for joy thereof goeth and selleth all that he hath, and buyeth that field.

This is the first of two very short parables given by the Lord as a general instruction concerning the discovery of the gospel.

The kingdom of heaven is here compared to a treasure hidden in a field. The man who discovers the treasure is not looking for it, but apparently stumbles upon it. There are only two ways to discover the gospel. One is by accident, as depicted here, wherein the individual is not looking for or struggling in any way to acquire the kingdom of heaven; the second way, referred to in the parable of the pearl of great price (see the following section), is represented by the individual who is diligently seeking the kingdom.

As the parable of the treasure hidden in a field progresses, it appears that in his first moments of discovery, the man fears that he might lose the treasure so recently uncovered, so he immediately hides the treasure and proceeds to acquire it by purchasing the field. The law and tradition of the time was in full accord with this procedure.[1] But this is not the point of the parable, and no emphasis should be placed here. Neither is there a question of morality involved in such a procedure. These were merely the trappings of the parabolic story, and they should be disregarded as unimportant to the parable's intended spiritual lessons.

The parable next discloses that the man goes with joy to purchase the field. The Lord had declared that the treasure was the kingdom of heaven (or the gospel), and the joy the man experienced upon such a valuable discovery is quite in harmony with the intent and meaning of the parable. For it was the man's discovery that precipitated his joy, that made him intent on acquiring the treasure, and that made him willing to pay the necessary price to obtain it.

The parable contains only two elements that require interpretation. The first is the discovery of the treasure and the immediate recognition of its inestimable value. This was a favorite theme in Oriental folklore,[2] and would have been readily recognized by the Lord's listeners. But it was not the ultimate purpose of the parable. The treasure, by definition, was the kingdom of heaven, and therefore, its worth was far beyond the worth of all treasures (since it is the most desirable of all treasures that can be acquired).

The second element of the parable to be interpreted was the requirement of the individual to acquire the valuable treasure once it had been found.[3] The Lord taught that principle when he declared that the man "selleth all that he hath, and buyeth that field." This is the requirement for those who discover the gospel. In the things of the world some are rich and some are poor, but the total value of their possessions does not matter, for it is required of those who discover the gospel to give *all* in order to possess it. The parable did not put a price on the treasure. It required that all things of the world be subjugated to the gospel to assure its acquisition.[4] The gospel is only obtained by the joyful self-sacrifice of all worldly things and the realization of the worthlessness of all human possessions in comparison.

Such a requirement has been vividly portrayed elsewhere in the scriptures. Jesus declared, "If any man will come after me, let him deny himself, and take up his cross, and follow me" (Matthew 16:24); "let the dead bury their dead" (Matthew 8:22); "No man, having put his hand to the plough, and looking back, is fit for the kingdom of God" (Luke 9:62); "If any man come to me, and hate not his father, and mother . . . he cannot be my disciple" (Luke 14:26); "sell that thou hast . . . and come and follow me" (Matthew 19:21). And in yet another place he indicated that it was better, figuratively speaking, to cut off a hand or a foot, or pluck out an eye, than to allow the worldly to overcome the spiritual (Mark 9:43–48). These teachings forcefully indicate the meaning of the parable. Once discovered, the kingdom was to be placed above all else.

A most interesting example of the discovery of the gospel is recorded in the fourth chapter of John. As Jesus was journeying through Samaria, he stopped and rested at the well Jacob had given his son Joseph. A woman appeared and drew water, and Jesus requested a drink from her. The woman was startled because Jesus was a Jew and she was a Samaritan. In response to the astonishment of the woman, Jesus questioned her: "If thou knewest the gift of God, and who it is that saith to thee, Give me to drink; thou wouldest have asked of him, and he would have given thee living water" (John 4:10). But the woman misunderstood and requested the Savior to give her this "living water" that she would thirst not. She had not yet discovered the kingdom, and thought only of the earthly requirement of the thirst of the body. Jesus continued his instruction and she, beginning to glimpse his meaning, declared that she was waiting for the

Messiah to come, who would be called Christ. Jesus then openly declared to her, "I that speak unto thee am he" (John 4:26).

The woman hurriedly returned to her village and declared to all she met that the Christ had come, and the people followed her out of the city to see the wonder she spoke of. By this time the disciples had returned to Jesus, and as the people approached he declared, "Lift up your eyes, and look on the fields; for they are white already to harvest" (John 4:35).

In their eagerness to acquire the treasure so recently found, the people requested that the Lord stay with them, and he spent two additional days there. They had discovered the gospel and wanted more of its teachings that they might enjoy its fulness, and the scripture declares that "many more believed because of his own word" (John 4:41).

These examples only emphasize the poignant meaning of the parable. The worth of the kingdom was obvious, but those who discovered it assumed an absolute obligation to acquire it and to set aside all worldly possessions and concerns in order to possess the previously hidden treasure.[5]

The Pearl of Great Price

Matthew 13:45–46

45. Again, the kingdom of heaven is like unto a merchant man, seeking goodly pearls:

46. Who, when he had found one pearl of great price, went and sold all that he had, and bought it.

With simplicity and beauty, the Lord used this parable to again point out what we should do once we have discovered the gospel. The parable of the treasure hidden in the field explained what the responsibility was for those who accidentally stumbled upon the kingdom. This parable, on the other hand, declares a similar responsibility for those who are actively seeking the kingdom of heaven and find it.

The parable begins by declaring that the kingdom of heaven is like unto a merchant man who was seeking goodly pearls. However, the kingdom of heaven in the parable is not symbolized by the merchant man, but by the pearl.[6] The merchant was a dealer in pearls, and he knew exactly what he was searching for. This situation is totally opposite to that of the man who accidentally stumbled upon the hidden treasure.

The value of the pearl the merchant was looking for is assumed, but it must be kept "in mind the esteem in which pearls were held in antiquity, so that there is record of almost incredible sums offered for single pearls, when perfect."[7]

The merchant, once he saw the perfect pearl, immediately recognized its value. This is directly comparable to those devoted investigators who search diligently for the kingdom of heaven.[8] They may not immediately discover the kingdom, but they have the necessary characteristics within their makeup to continue the quest until the kingdom is found.

There is no surprise implied in this parable, as there is in the treasure hidden in the field, for the merchant knows exactly what he is searching for; and once the priceless pearl is identified, the merchant knows exactly what he must do to acquire it. The price is the same as it was for the hidden treasure, and the merchant sold all that he had in order to obtain the pearl.

Once again it is made clear that the kingdom must be acquired with *all* that we have, whether we are actively in search of it or stumble upon it accidentally. Once we discover the gospel, we must part with all else that would conflict or be foreign to it.[9] This does not necessarily mean that we must deprive ourselves of our earthly possessions, but it does mean that the Lord and the gospel come before the things of the world. We may be required to give up old ways, and perhaps change our minds about certain doctrines or acquired beliefs. The seeker may, as Paul declares, have to reject certain philosophies or "science falsely so called" (1 Timothy 6:20) in order to acquire the pearl.

The story of Christ's encounter with the rich young man (see Matthew 19:16–27) exemplifies this parable's teaching. The rich man could not bring himself to sacrifice his wealth and follow the Savior. The Apostles, on the other hand, had "forsaken all." They had done what the rich man could not—they had paid the price and purchased the pearl. Because of their willingness to follow the Lord, they were promised the reward. They would be with him in his glory and would "sit upon twelve thrones" (Matthew 19:28).

The conclusion is simple: When we are willing to give our all for the kingdom, the kingdom will be ours.[10]

Lost and Then Found 4

The gospel Jesus taught provided the way into the kingdom of God. The way was straight and narrow, and the requirements explicit. "I am the way, the truth, and the life," he said, "no man cometh unto the Father, but by me" (John 14:6). All who heard his words had the freedom of choice to accept or reject them, but the meaning was clear: without the gospel, entrance into the kingdom was impossible.

Once the kingdom was accepted, freedom of choice continued. In the following parables the Lord taught of those who, for whatever reason, failed to keep the requirements of the kingdom and became lost, and of the leadership's responsibility to them.

The Lost Sheep

Luke 15:1—7

1. Then drew near unto him all the publicans and sinners for to hear him.

2. And the Pharisees and scribes murmured, saying, This man receiveth sinners, and eateth with them.

3. And he spake this parable unto them, saying,

4. What man of you,

having an hundred sheep, if
he lose one of them, doth
not leave the ninety and
nine in the wilderness, and
go after that which is lost,
until he find it?
5. And when he hath
found it, he layeth it on his
shoulders, rejoicing.
6. And when he cometh
home, he calleth together his
friends and neighbours,
saying unto them, Rejoice
with me; for I have found
my sheep which was lost.
7. I say unto you, that
likewise joy shall be in
heaven over one sinner that
repenteth, more than over
ninety and nine just persons,
which need no repentance.

Cross-reference

Matthew 18:12–14

The parable of the lost sheep is recorded twice in the scriptures. Its interpretation, although generally the same in both instances, was applied to two widely differing groups of people: enemies in Luke, friends in Matthew.

Luke records that Jesus was teaching a group of publicans and sinners who had come to hear him, and the Pharisees and scribes murmured, saying, "This man receiveth sinners, and eateth with them." The Lord answered the accusation by teaching a sequence of parables beginning with the lost sheep, continuing on to the lost coin, and ending with the prodigal son.

The Pharisees, scribes, and rulers of the Jews despised the publicans and sinners. In their self-righteousness, they considered themselves superior. Their self-aggrandizement had risen to such heights that they felt no need for repentance, believing that they had committed no sin; therefore, they felt the association of publicans and sinners would defile them, making them unworthy for the kingdom of God.[1]

Publicans, considered sinners, were accounted as traitors, "who for the sake of filthy lucre had sided with the Romans, the oppressors of the theocracy, and now collected for a heathen treasury. No alms might be received from their money chest; their evidence was not taken in courts of justice, and they were put on the same level with heathens."[2]

The Pharisees and scribes were accounted as the keepers of the covenant, protectors of the law, possessors of the kingdom—

the shepherds of Israel. Now, however, the true Shepherd of Israel stood before them. These erstwhile shepherds had long since ignored their lost sheep. While forsaking their duty, they rejoiced in the "evil" of the publicans and sinners and were thankful that they themselves were not one of them.[3] But Ezekiel had seen their day and had issued this warning to them: "Son of man, prophesy against the shepherds of Israel, prophesy, and say unto them, Thus saith the Lord God unto the shepherds; Woe be to the shepherds of Israel that do feed themselves! should not the shepherds feed the flocks? Ye eat the fat, and ye clothe you with the wool, ye kill them that are fed: but ye feed not the flock." (Ezekiel 34:2–3.)

Zechariah further emphasized this warning and prophesied:

> For, lo, I will raise up a shepherd in the land, which shall not visit those that be cut off, neither shall seek the young one, nor heal that that is broken, nor feed that that standeth still: but he shall eat the flesh of the fat, and tear their claws in pieces. Woe to the idol shepherd that leaveth the flock! the sword shall be upon his arm, and upon his right eye: his arm shall be clean dried up, and his right eye shall be utterly darkened. (Zechariah 11:16–17.)

The prophesied criticism of the "shepherds" of Israel had come to pass. Now the Pharisees and scribes were finding fault with Jesus for doing the very thing that they should have been doing. Jesus offered the gospel to both shepherd and sheep alike. But the shepherds, in their self-righteous condition, had refused association with the sheep, whom they considered "sinners." They took offense at Jesus, for he received lost souls graciously and lived in close association with them, while they themselves "had neither love to hope for the recovery of such, nor medicines to effect it."[4]

The ninety-nine sheep in this parable are described as those "just persons, which need no repentance." Perhaps they were righteous partakers of the gospel who did not need immediate attention, but perhaps rather the Master meant them to represent the very critics then confronting him,[5] since this parable was given in response to the murmurings of the Pharisees and scribes. They relished the Law and their cold, self-righteous correctness within it. If you (the Pharisees and Sadducees) are "in the sheepfold, I have no mission for you," the Lord was saying to them, for "I am sent to look up sheep that are lost," these you have "despised."[6]

The "one lost sheep" in the parable was representative of those publicans and sinners who had drifted away from the Law, and were excluded, avoided, and shunned by the very keepers of it. It was to these errant souls that Jesus extended the glad tidings of the gospel while reemphasizing the leadership's obligation to seek out and recover those Israelites who had been spiritually lost. It was their duty to recover these souls, not to rejoice over their evil and ostracize them from the religious community. The joy expressed in the parable resulted from the recovery (through repentance) of the sheep that was lost.[7]

In Matthew's account the circumstances that led to the use of this parable was quite different. In Luke, the Lord was speaking to the self-righteous rulers of the Jews who had rejected him and become his most bitter enemies. But in Matthew he was speaking to his disciples, followers of the word, eager for instruction. Yet the question they asked Jesus exemplified the same attitude as that of the Pharisees and scribes in Luke. To Jesus they said, "Who is the greatest in the kingdom of heaven?" (Matthew 18:1.)

The nuances of the Law, as taught by the Pharisees and rulers of the Jews, had given rise to a desire for personal aggrandizement and a separation of classes among the Jews. Jesus did not want the errors of the old Law to creep into the new. He prefaced the answer to his disciples' question with an analogy of little children: "Whosoever therefore shall humble himself as this little child, the same is greatest in the kingdom of heaven" (Matthew 18:4). He then continued with a discussion on offenses, and the need to eliminate them, as he declared, "For the Son of man is come to save that which was lost" (Matthew 18:11). It was at this juncture that he delivered the parable of the lost sheep. He made it clear that the shepherds of the new gospel, as well as those of the old Law, were responsible to look after the Lord's sheep.

The one lost sheep underlined the value of each member of the flock in the eyes of the Father. If one were lost, it was God's will that the leadership should go after him, and his repentance would bring great joy to all.

This parable is an outstanding example of the Lord's use of parables. It applied to both enemy and friend. To the Pharisees, who believed that "there is joy before God when those who provoke Him perish from the world,"[8] it pointed out that there was greater rejoicing over a repentant sinner than over those who were adhering strictly to the Law.

This parable taught the Apostles that their ascension to leadership in the Church should facilitate not only the gathering of souls into the kingdom of God, but the retention of those souls within the kingdom. For it is "not the will of your Father which is in heaven, that one of these little ones should perish" (Matthew 18:14).

One last, important point can be drawn from this parable. The sheep that was lost had *strayed* from the flock. It is natural for sheep to wander, and as they drift farther and farther they eventually are lost from the safety of the flock and are unable to find their way back without a diligent search on the part of the shepherd. When a diligent search proves successful, however, and the sheep is found, he will be joyously returned to the flock in full fellowship and accord.

The Lost Coin

Luke 15:8—10

8. Either what woman having ten pieces of silver, if she lose one piece, doth not light a candle, and sweep the house, and seek diligently till she find it?

9. And when she hath found it, she calleth her friends and her neighbours together, saying, Rejoice with me; for I have found the piece which I had lost.

10. Likewise, I say unto you, there is joy in the presence of the angels of God over one sinner that repenteth.

The parables of the lost sheep and the lost coin appear similar on the surface, but it would be incorrect to assume that they say exactly the same thing. The Lord's teachings, initiated in the parable of the lost sheep, are expanded in the parable of the lost coin, and expanded still further in the parable of the prodigal son. In these parables it appears that the Lord is teaching these two things simultaneously and progressively: (1) the responsibility of leadership toward errant individuals within the covenant, gospel, or Church, and (2) the responsibility of the wayward individual toward the covenant, gospel, or Church.

A comparison of the parable of the lost sheep with that of the lost coin is helpful in defining and discussing the simultaneous and expanded teachings:

Lost Sheep	Lost Coin
• *Individual* wanders	• *Individual* negligently loses coin
• Accepted back (repentance assumed)	• Accepted back (repentance emphasized)
• Blessings restored	• Blessings restored
• Attitude: disinterested	• Attitude: negligent
• *Leadership* responsibility for loss undefined	• *Leadership* responsible for loss
• Leaves to find	• Diligent search required
• Discovers: brings back to flock	• Recovers through diligent search
• Rejoices at finding	• Rejoices at finding

In the parable of the lost sheep, the flock represents the chosen people within the covenant, gospel, or Church; the shepherd represents the Jewish leadership; and the lost sheep represents the errant individual. But in the lost coin the parabolic players become more complicated and assume dual roles as the Lord expands the teaching. The woman plays the role of the shepherd when she is the keeper of the coin, but she also portrays the errant individual who has lost the gospel. The coin also takes on two identities, representing the wayward sheep entrusted to the Church when the woman represents the shepherd; and the gospel itself when the woman represents the errant individual. The parable of the lost coin was specifically directed to the Pharisees and Sadducees as the leadership of Israel, but it can be applied to any of the authorized leaders of the Church in any age.[9]

While it is clear in the parable of the lost sheep that both the leadership and the individual have undefined and perhaps limited responsibility in the separation of the sheep from the flock, this is clearly not so in the lost coin. The coin was lost solely through the negligence of the woman;[10] thus separation from the Church can come through the negligence of the leadership (Jesus denounced the Jewish leadership on several occasions for this very sin—see, for example, Luke 11:37–51; Matthew 23) or the negligence of the individual.

In the parable of the lost sheep, the sinner merely strayed from the Lord in the normal course of life's events, whereas in the lost coin, the sinner was lost as a result of *culpability* and *negligence.* The owner of the coin recognized immediately that something valuable had been lost and needed to be recovered. This fact is stressed in the parable, for the emphasis immediately focuses on the search for the coin.[11] The recovery of the lost sheep was simple and uncomplicated, but not so with the coin. Negligent loss requires diligent seeking.

The first thing the woman in the parable did was find a candle so that she could search past the normal daylight hours and probe into every darkened corner of her house. She meticulously swept the house, undoubtedly searching the furniture and even moving it to be certain the search would be complete. The woman's diligence in attempting to find the coin directly relates to both the effort required of the leadership to recover lost souls for the Lord, and the individual's effort, through repentance, to return to the fold.

When the woman finds the coin she rejoices, and even invites her neighbors in to share her happiness. Anyone who has been influential in changing a person's life for good can relate to these feelings. Similarly there is joy in heaven over one recovered soul or one repentant sinner.

Through these two succinct parables (the lost sheep and the lost coin), the leadership of the Church was admonished in their responsibility toward lost souls and the individual was admonished in his responsibility toward the gospel. The third parable, that of the prodigal son, will graphically depict what happens when an individual leaves the fold deliberately—as a result of choice. Although the leadership's responsibility is again elaborated upon, the main emphasis of the prodigal son shifts from the responsibility of the leaders to the responsibility of the individual.

The Prodigal Son

Luke 15:11–32

11. And he said, A certain man had two sons:
12. And the younger of them said to his father, Father, give me the portion of goods that falleth to me. And he divided unto them his living.
13. And not many days after the younger son gathered all together, and took his journey into a far country, and there wasted his substance with riotous living.
14. And when he had spent all, there arose a mighty famine in that land; and he began to be in want.
15. And he went and joined himself to a citizen of that country; and he sent him into his fields to feed swine.
16. And he would fain have filled his belly with the husks that the swine did eat: and no man gave unto him.
17. And when he came to himself, he said, How many hired servants of my father's have bread enough and to spare, and I perish with hunger!
18. I will arise and go to my father, and will say unto him, Father, I have sinned against heaven, and before thee,
19. And am no more worthy to be called thy son: make me as one of thy hired servants.
20. And he arose, and came to his father. But when he was yet a great way off, his father saw him, and had compassion, and ran, and fell on his neck, and kissed him.
21. And the son said unto him, Father, I have sinned against heaven, and in thy sight, and am no more worthy to be called thy son.
22. But the father said to his servants, Bring forth the best robe, and put it on him; and put a ring on his hand, and shoes on his feet:
23. And bring hither the fatted calf, and kill it; and let us eat, and be merry:
24. For this my son was dead, and is alive again; he was lost, and is found. And they began to be merry.

25. Now his elder son
was in the field: and as he
came and drew nigh to the
house, he heard musick and
dancing.
26. And he called one of
the servants, and asked what
these things meant.
27. And he said unto
him, Thy brother is come;
and thy father hath killed
the fatted calf, because he
hath received him safe and
sound.
28. And he was angry,
and would not go in: therefore came his father out, and
intreated him.
29. And he answering
said to his father, Lo, these
many years do I serve thee,
neither transgressed I at any
time thy commandment: and
yet thou never gavest me a
kid, that I might make
merry with my friends:
30. But as soon as this
thy son was come, which
hath devoured thy living
with harlots, thou hast killed
for him the fatted calf.
31. And he said unto
him, Son, thou art ever with
me, and all that I have is
thine.
32. It was meet that we
should make merry, and be
glad: for this thy brother
was dead, and is alive again;
and was lost, and is found.

The prodigal son is one of the most moving and enlightening parables in the Bible. It is a parable of heavenly doctrine that draws its comparisons from real-life situations. Meaning does not need to be forced upon this parable, for its setting was completely understandable to the Jews, as was its heavenly application.[12]

The parables of the lost sheep and the lost coin gave instructions to the leaders of the Jews that centered on their responsibility toward the wayward souls of the Church, whether those souls had merely wandered away or were lost through negligence. However, in the prodigal son the leadership is depicted as having successfully completed its responsibility to the individual. The individual is already an heir to the Lord's blessings and is lost through *deliberate choice*—he willfully chooses to separate himself from the flock.

Two sons are described in this parable. The younger son impatiently asks his father for an early inheritance, desiring to use his wealth immediately. He does not want to wait until his father's death. The father consents to his request, and divides to him his portion of the inheritance.

The son does not immediately leave after receiving his goods. He lingers several days in order to gather together all that he has, so that he will be adequately prepared for his journey into the world. He then leaves for a far country where he can forget both God and father.[13]

The emphasis of the parable at this point is clear. The son deliberately chooses to separate himself from his father. The father in this case may be interpreted as representing either God or the Church (the consequences being the same in either case).

The Lord had now expanded his teachings, with regard to the individual's responsibility to the gospel, to include all the methods of losing it. In the lost sheep the loss occurred inadvertently, the soul simply strayed away. In the lost coin, the soul was lost through culpable negligence. But in the prodigal son, the soul deliberately chose to leave the Church.

An Old Testament story that has some similarities with that of the prodigal son is the story of Esau and Jacob. Esau, the twin brother of Jacob, had returned from a long hunt and was faint. He asked Jacob to feed him some of the pottage that Jacob had prepared. Jacob agreed, but first requested that Esau sell him his birthright to pay for the food. Esau decided that his hunger was such that he would die if he did not immediately receive nourishment, and he said, "What profit shall this birthright do to me?" (Genesis 25:32.) He sold Jacob his birthright for the bowl of pottage.

So also the prodigal son willfully desired to exchange his inheritance for the things of the world. He spent his inheritance, never to recover it. The parable reports that he wasted his substance with "riotous living." He lost his kingdom by succumbing to the bondage of the world, his own lusts, and the tyranny of the devil.[14]

Undoubtedly when the prodigal first departed from the safety of the fold the attractions and pleasures of the world gave him satisfaction, and he probably congratulated himself on his newfound liberty and worldly enjoyment. But eventually his inheritance was dissipated, and the time came when the creature delights of his worldly passions forsook him. His desperate circumstances made him recognize the true calamity of his departure from the kingdom (see Jeremiah 2:19, 17:5—6).

He had spent all of his inheritance when there arose a mighty famine in the land. With no funds to provide for himself, the prodigal began to want. He hired out to a citizen of the country in which he was residing, and was given the task of feeding the swine in the fields. The cup of his misery and despair was full. He did not have enough to eat, no one would help him, and he had sunk so low that he "would fain have filled his belly with the husks that the swine did eat."

The prodigal's situation was graphically described by the Savior. He made it clear in the parable that those who would not be ruled by God would find themselves serving Satan. The prodigal son had squandered his inheritance through sin and had debased himself into the depths of hell. But adversity proved to be a powerful prodder, and he suddenly recognized that even the hired servants in his father's house had bread to eat, while he perished with hunger. He decided to return to his father, admit that he had sinned against him and heaven, openly avow that he was no more worthy to be his son, and request that his father let him be one of the hired servants. With this in mind, he returned to his father's house, where he was undoubtedly overwhelmed to be received openly and joyously, and have all his *earthly* needs abundantly provided for. His candid confession and his recognition of disobedience proclaimed his future state. He had rejected his home and squandered his inheritance. He knew that he could no longer be a son. He would have to be satisfied with what his father gave him; we cannot make inference from this parable that the repentant sinner will be given precedence over a righteous soul who has consistently lived the gospel throughout his life.[15] Clearly this is not the case.

The Lord now interjects into this parable the anger of the first son who had served faithfully through the years, as was his duty. Even though he had conscientiously fulfilled his obligations to his father, he had not received any of the attention now being showered upon his errant younger brother.

At this juncture, the emphasis of the parable shifts. No longer is the returning son the center of attention. The first son now takes center stage. The younger son had lived but for today, deliberately rejecting his eternal inheritance in the kingdom to satisfy his immediate, earthly desires and passions. His inheritance had been dissipated, and he would never enjoy it again.[16] The father assured the faithful, older son that he was ever with him, and all that the father had was his. On the other hand, the prodigal would never enter into the fullness of the father's kingdom, but would indeed participate only as a servant. He would not share again in that which he had rejected.[17]

No emphasis need be laid upon the apparent dissatisfaction of the elder brother because of the celebration given at the return of the prodigal son. This information probably was only parabolic dressing intended to define the relationship between the brothers and their position in the kingdom of God.

Undoubtedly the Lord's disciples were with him as he taught the parables of the sheep, coin, and prodigal son, but the rest of his audience was comprised of sinners and outcasts of the Jewish people, as well as the critical rulers of the Jews. In these three parables the Lord implicitly revealed to this audience what their responsibility was in the kingdom of God once they had discovered it. The contest, after all, is a contest of faith, and only our faith in God makes us strong enough to be victorious over the things of the world.

Anciently, the children of Israel exemplified this principle when they petitioned Samuel to approach the Lord to have him "make us a king to judge us like all the nations" (1 Samuel 8:5). Samuel was displeased with their request, and prayed to the Lord for direction. The Lord, in his response, confirmed Samuel's displeasure and said, "For they have not rejected thee, but they have rejected me" (1 Samuel 8:7). (So, likewise, had the prodigal son rejected the kingdom of God.) Saul was then selected to be the first king of Israel, and he determined to be the kind of king Israel wanted, but this was not what the Lord wanted. He did not have sufficient faith in the Lord, and his weakness made him bow to a wicked people. Saul's kingdom was not of God, and therefore it could not continue.

Even though their circumstances were different, Saul became as unfit for his kingship as Esau was for the inheritance rights of a firstborn son, or as the prodigal son was for the inheritance he received from his father. Whatever qualifications they may have originally had for the kingdom, they all rejected them to satisfy their own desires for a worldly existence. They rejected the kingdom willingly and knowingly, and openly dissipated their inheritance. The blessings of the kingdom are assured only to those who remain faithful to the Lord.

The responsibility of the individual to the gospel was clearly presented to those who heard the parable of the prodigal son. The parables of the pearl of great price and the treasure hidden in the field determined that a person must readily sacrifice all he has in order to acquire the gospel. The parables of the lost sheep and the lost coin dictated that those who inadvertently or negligently found themselves separated from the gospel could rightfully return upon complete repentance. Just as plain is the reality that if the gospel is wholly accepted and then completely rejected, willfully, knowledgeably, and permanently, the rewards of the kingdom cannot be obtained, and inheritance in the Father's kingdom will be forfeit.[18]

Part Three

Teaching Principles and Relationships

Teaching Gospel Principles 5

Implicit in all the teachings of the gospel are the principles that form its foundation. They provide the guidelines that constitute the fundamental policies of Christ's instruction. He taught these principles in everything he did. His daily activities exemplified them, his love of children emphasized them, his discourses described them, and his miracles provided visual evidence of their importance, truth, and divinity.

The principles of the gospel were the "weightier" matters of the law, and had been forgotten or ignored through the ritualistic observance of the Law of Moses. Through these principles the Lord taught the importance of the spirit of the law as well as the letter of the law. This chapter deals with the parables that taught these important principles.

Prayer

The Importunate Widow (The Unjust Judge)

Luke 18:1–5

1. And he spake a parable unto them to this end, that men ought always to pray, and not to faint;

2. Saying, There was in a city a judge, which feared not God, neither regarded man:

3. And there was a widow in that city; and she came unto him, saying, Avenge me of mine adversary.

4. And he would not for a while: but afterward he said within himself, Though I fear not God, nor regard man;

5. Yet because this widow troubleth me, I will avenge her, lest by her continual coming she weary me.

Luke states that this parable was given to show "that men ought always to pray, and not to faint." It teaches the principle of prayer. However, it is not a parable on how to pray, but one that tells us we should pray—not out of duty, but out of necessity. The characters in the parable perfectly emphasize the principle.

The first character is the judge. The Lord accentuated his independence from all of the normal influences that affect daily activities by stating that this judge "feared not God, neither regarded man." These words would have been recognized by the Jews as describing a person of "utterly unprincipled character."[1] By this it was evident that the judge would give only those judgments that he wished to give or that would enhance his chosen position. He did not fear retribution from God for unjust judgments, and his power was so strongly consolidated that he feared no man. Although he is the main character in the parable, his position should not be compared to that of Christ or the Father.[2] He is merely parabolic dressing to emphasize the principle being taught.

The second character is the widow. She petitions the judge to avenge her of an adversary. She is also parabolic dressing and she does not correlate to any higher meaning. She is a foil to the judge. She emphasizes his power, and represents the most defenseless and helpless of individuals in the real-life situations of Jesus' time.[3] (See Isaiah 1:23; Matthew 23:14.) The more unjust the judge, the more helpless the widow. The more indifferent to God and man the judge is, the less apt the widow is to receive her petition from him. These comparisons help to emphasize the point of the parable.

The poor widow's first petition to the judge went unanswered, but eventually he relented and came to the conclusion that he should answer her, not because he feared God nor regarded man, but "because this widow troubleth me, . . . lest by her continual coming she weary me." It was not that her petition was just, nor that the judge of necessity must respond to it; but he was tired of her perpetual nagging. Therefore, to rid himself of the widow he decided to grant her petition.

The setting in this parable emphasized the following teachings on prayer.

Persistence. It is obvious from the story that the widow persisted in her petition to the unjust judge. We are not told whether her petition was a righteous one, although it may be assumed that such was the case. From this we can conclude that our own prayers to God should be persistent in righteous purposes. It is not the intention of the parable to teach that persistence in prayer will always bring the answer we seek; but only that we should pray persistently and continually to our Father in Heaven.[4]

There may be times when prayer is more fervent or intense than others, but it might be argued from the parable that our prayers should not be limited to those intense times when our need of heavenly assistance is crucial and urgent. For instance, we should also be persistent in seeking long-term blessings and in giving thanks for blessings granted. Prayer of this type is a proper exercise of our faith in our Father in Heaven,[5] and it further fulfills the instructions of the Savior that we should ask if we desire to receive, we should seek if we desire to find, and we should knock if we desire to have the door opened (see Matthew 7:8; 3 Nephi 14:8; Moroni 7:26).

It would appear from the parable that if we are persistent in prayer, it will automatically lead to the reward sought. But it is more probable that the idea of persistence was taught to provoke man to recognize his constant need to rely on his Father in Heaven, "even when all around seems to forbid the hope of answer."[6]

Patience. The widow continually petitioned for redress. She was patient in those petitions, anticipating their eventual granting, even though the circumstances and the power of the judge seemed to discourage the hope of such. The Lord expects us to continue in patient prayer for as long as it takes to gain the answer we need,[7] even though it may seem that God is deaf to our pleas and petitions.[8] In this manner we evidence our faith to the true and living God.

An interesting miracle occurred in the Lord's ministry which emphasized these two principles of persistence and patience. This was the miracle of the healing of the Syrophenician's daughter.[9]

In this miracle a woman, who was a heathen, petitioned the Lord to heal her daughter who was grievously vexed with a devil. But the Lord did not immediately answer her. Her petitions continued and the Apostles came to the Lord and besought him to send her away, for she continued to cry after them and was apparently an embarrassment to them. The Lord then turned his attention to the woman and told her that he had been sent only to the lost sheep of the house of Israel. Not to be deterred, she immediately worshipped him and continued to earnestly seek his help. The Lord turned to her and said, "It is not meet to take the children's bread, and to cast it to dogs" (Matthew 15:26). But the woman would not be denied. She persisted and responded, "Yet the dogs eat of the crumbs which fall from their masters' table" (Matthew 15:27). Jesus immediately recognized the great faith of the woman, and granted her petition.

The woman in the miracle of the Syrophenician's daughter is comparable to the importunate widow. Her petition was righteous. She desired a healing for her daughter. She persisted in her petition and by so doing demonstrated the great faith and patience that she had in the Lord. The disciples did not immediately recognize this, and the Lord instructed them as well as the woman as he granted her petition.

The Lord himself concluded the parable of the importunate widow by emphasizing the principle it contained. He declared: "Hear what the unjust judge saith. And shall not God avenge his own elect, which cry day and night unto him, though he bear long with them? I tell you that he will avenge them speedily. Nevertheless when the Son of man cometh, shall he find faith on the earth?" (Luke 18:6–8.) A loving God will grant the desires of those faithful souls who persistently petition their righteous needs before him and await patiently his response.[10]

The Friend at Midnight (The Importuned Friend)

Luke 11:5–10

5. And he said unto them, Which of you shall have a friend, and shall go unto him at midnight, and say unto him, Friend, lend me three loaves;

6. For a friend of mine in his journey is come to me, and I have nothing to set before him?

7. And he from within shall answer and say, Trouble me not: the door is now shut, and my children are with me in bed; I cannot rise and give thee.

8. I say unto you, Though he will not rise and give him, because he is his friend, yet because of his importunity he will rise and give him as many as he needeth.

9. And I say unto you, Ask, and it shall be given you; seek, and ye shall find; knock, and it shall be opened unto you.

10. For every one that asketh receiveth; and he that seeketh findeth; and to him that knocketh it shall be opened.

This parable was given as a result of the disciples' request that Jesus teach them how to pray. The Lord began his instruction by giving them the example of the Lord's prayer, and then he taught them this parable, which again emphasizes the necessity of enduring, persistent prayer.

Unlike the importunate widow (in which the participants were antagonistic toward each other), here the participants are friends. The principle the Lord is teaching occurs within the framework of the parable rather than the conversation between the parties.

A man asks his friend to loan him three loaves of bread. How often have we gone to neighbors and friends to borrow what we lack in times of need? But the importance of the parable was not simply in the borrowing, it was in the late hour that the petition was made. The man does not go to borrow during the normal daylight hours but extends his plea at midnight, long after his friend has retired. Thus the request appears unreasonable, and the man could not be sure that his friend would help him.[11]

The request itself was not unjust. The hospitality of the

Jewish social system of the time required that a friend lay food before his visitor, and that a neighbor assist in said courtesy if necessary.[12] But these normal rules of hospitality were waived in this parable because of the unreasonable hour.

The neighbor, awakened by the knocking, denied the man's request, indicating that his doors were shut and his children and family all in bed.

The man continued to plead his just cause. Finally, the friend within arose and unbolted the door, not only because he was a friend, but because he was being strongly persuaded. He gave the man not just that which he requested, but all that was needed. "The Lord's lesson was, that if man, with all his selfishness and disinclination to give, will nevertheless grant what his neighbor with proper purpose asks and continues to ask in spite of objection and temporary refusal, with assured certainty will God grant what is persistently asked in faith and with righteous intent."[13]

Through this parable the Lord instructs us to "ask" in earnestness, believing that a response will be received. He expects us to "seek," not halfheartedly, but energetically and persistently, and to "knock" intently and loudly.[14]

Many things can get in the way of our receiving an answer to prayer. Sometimes the Father delays granting our petitions so that our asking will be more fervent.[15] In this parable the persistence of the man overcame the reluctance of his ungracious friend. How much more shall our persistence prevail with our Father in Heaven, "who loves us better than we ourselves, and who is more ready to hear than we to pray."[16]

An example from the Old Testament illustrates this righteous petitioning of the Lord.[17] The Lord stood before Abraham and declared that he would destroy Sodom and Gomorrah because of their grievous sins before him. Abraham, knowing that his nephew Lot and Lot's family were in the city, drew near to the Lord and questioned whether he would destroy the righteous along with the wicked. His earnest persistence came in the form of bargaining. He asked the Lord if He would spare the city if he could find fifty righteous souls. The Lord agreed that if fifty righteous souls could be found within the city, he would spare it for their sakes. But there were not fifty members in Lot's family, so Abraham again petitioned the Lord and asked if forty-five righteous souls would suffice. Again the Lord agreed, but forty-five could not be found; so the bartering continued from forty righteous to thirty, down to twenty, and even ten. But there were not ten righteous souls to be found in all the environs of Sodom and Gomorrah, so the Lord had Lot and his family removed from the city before he destroyed it (Genesis 18:20—33; 19:15—25).

Although there were not a sufficient number of righteous souls to convince the Lord to spare the city, this incident still exemplifies the principle taught in the parable of the friend at midnight. A petition was righteously made and persistently followed up. It would have been granted had the conditions been met.

The parable of the friend at midnight taught the disciples a simple lesson on prayer. Prayer was not to be merely repetitious; believing souls needed sincerity and perseverance to acquire answers and blessings, both for themselves and others. If they are couched in faith and trust, God will assuredly hear our petitions.[18] The Lord strongly emphasized this point to his disciples when he declared: "If a son shall ask bread of any of you that is a father, will he give him a stone? or if he ask a fish, will he for a fish give him a serpent? Or if he shall ask an egg, will he offer him a scorpion? If ye then, being evil, know how to give good gifts unto your children: how much more shall your heavenly Father give the Holy Spirit to them that ask him?" (Luke 11:11—13.)

Obedience

The Two Sons

Matthew 21:28—32

28. But what think ye? A certain man had two sons; and he came to the first, and said, Son, go work to day in my vineyard.

29. He answered and said, I will not: but afterward he repented, and went.

30. And he came to the second, and said likewise. And he answered and said, I go, sir: and went not.

31. Whether of them twain did the will of his father? They say unto him, The first. Jesus saith unto

them, Verily I say unto you, That the publicans and the harlots go into the kingdom of God before you.

32. For John came unto you in the way of righteousness, and ye believed him not: but the publicans and the harlots believed him: and ye, when ye had seen it, repented not afterward, that ye might believe him.

This is one of those parables which draw their importance and meaning from the circumstances in which they are set. It is a parable of moral criticism, given during the last week of the ministry of Jesus as he taught in the temple.

Several important events had occurred just before Jesus gave this parable. He had returned to Jerusalem for the last time. On his way he had passed through Jericho, where two blind men sitting by the roadside had publicly acclaimed him as the Son of David (Matthew 20:29–34; Mark 10:46–52; Luke 18:35–43).[19] Then came his triumphant entry into Jerusalem, where the multitudes likewise proclaimed him king (Matthew 21:1–11; Mark 11:1–10; Luke 19:29–38). After entering Jerusalem, he cleansed the temple for the second and last time (Matthew 21:12–13; Mark 11:15–18; Luke 19:45–48). These public demonstrations greatly disturbed the Pharisees, and they came to him seeking a public disavowal, but he would not accommodate them (Matthew 21:15–16). They had previously asked him, "If thou be the Christ, tell us plainly" (John 10:24). He had confirmed that he was the Messiah, and they "took up stones again to stone him" (John 10:31).

Now the chief priests and the elders of the people again came to him as he was teaching in the temple and questioned his authority. They said, "By what authority doest thou these things? and who gave thee this authority?" (Matthew 21:23.)

Jesus took this last opportunity to offer the kingdom of God to the rulers of the Jews who had so openly rejected him and fought his ministry. He bargained with them, agreeing to reveal the source of his authority if they would answer a question. "The baptism of John," he said, "whence was it? from heaven, or of men?" (Matthew 21:25.)

The obdurate rulers reasoned among themselves, noting that if they answered that the authority of John was from heaven,

Jesus would ask them why they had not believed him; however, if they claimed John's authority was of man, they feared the reaction of the people, for the people accepted John as a prophet. And so they hedged and answered, "We cannot tell." Jesus then replied, "Neither tell I you by what authority I do these things" (Matthew 21:27).

The parable of the two sons was directed to these disbelieving and rebellious rulers of Israel, that they might have one more chance to open their eyes, recognize their false position, and accept Jesus as the Messiah.[20] They were on the verge of rejecting him totally, a sin of monumental proportions, and through this parable the Lord gave them opportunity to see the seriousness of what they were doing and repent of their transgressions.

This was a simple parable. A father had two sons. He asked the first to go and work in his vineyard and the boy initially refused, but afterward repented and went to do the work his father requested. The second son was asked to do the same work. He readily responded that he would go, but went not.

The first son in the parable represented the publicans and harlots, those of the chosen people who had been given the Mosiac Law, but openly transgressed it. They refused the call of the Father because of their careless and reckless life of sin. However, in the parable they recognized their sin, repented of their transgressions, and went to work in the vineyard as the Father had requested. The second son represented the Pharisees and other rulers of the Jews, those who professed righteous zeal for the Law. But they refused the truth when it was offered to them.[21] Their zeal for the Law had made them self-righteous to the point that the Lord referred to them as whited sepulchres, which outwardly appeared beautiful, but inwardly were full of dead men's bones and all uncleanliness (Matthew 23:27).

Jesus did not immediately declare the moral of his parable to them, but first asked them another question. "Whether of them twain [the sons in the parable] did the will of his father?" Unaccustomed to such candid questioning before the people, the Pharisees were left with only one possible answer, and they entrapped themselves by responding, "The first."[22] Now Jesus directly applied the parable to their situation. He told them that the publicans and the harlots would go into the kingdom of God before the Pharisees and the rulers of the Jews. He then referred back to the question of John's authority, which had prompted the parable in the first place. John came in the cause of righteousness, he declared, and the Pharisees and rulers believed him not. They, the protectors of the covenant, had seen the righteousness of John's teachings, but had rejected them and would not repent. Yet the publicans, harlots, and sinners had accepted and believed. The parable points out that sins of both commission and omission are possible. Those who repent and accept the gospel are readily accepted by God into his kingdom. Those who do not repent, yet profess obedience to the call of the Father, while refusing to do the simple things required, are rejected (even though they may be holders of the covenant).[23]

As Jesus continued his teaching, the chief priests and Pharisees "perceived that he spake of them" (Matthew 21:45). They wanted to restrain Jesus but they were afraid, for the people thought of him as a prophet.

The lesson of this parable is clear. We must be obedient to the Lord if we are to regain his kingdom. Some may initially reject the gospel but later accept it; if they sincerely repent they can still achieve the goal of salvation. However, those who profess obedience and acceptance of the Lord's call, yet do not magnify it, will surely be rejected.

Forgiveness

The Two Debtors

Luke 7:36—50

36. And one of the Pharisees desired him that he would eat with him. And he went into the Pharisee's house, and sat down to meat.

37. And, behold, a woman in the city, which was a sinner, when she knew that Jesus sat at meat in the Pharisee's house, brought an alabaster box of ointment.

38. And stood at his feet behind him weeping, and began to wash his feet with tears, and did wipe them with the hairs of her head,

and kissed his feet, and anointed them with the ointment.

39. Now when the Pharisee which had bidden him saw it, he spake within himself, saying, This man, if he were a prophet, would have known who and what manner of woman this is that toucheth him: for she is a sinner.

40. And Jesus answering said unto him, Simon, I have somewhat to say unto thee. And he saith, Master, say on.

41. There was a certain creditor which had two debtors: the one owed five hundred pence, and the other fifty.

42. And when they had nothing to pay, he frankly forgave them both. Tell me therefore, which of them will love him most?

43. Simon answered and said, I suppose that he, to whom he forgave most. And he said unto him, Thou hast rightly judged.

44. And he turned to the woman, and said unto Simon, Seest thou this woman? I entered into thine house, thou gavest me no water for my feet: but she hath washed my feet with tears, and wiped them with the hairs of her head.

45. Thou gavest me no kiss: but this woman since the time I came in hath not ceased to kiss my feet.

46. My head with oil thou didst not anoint: but this woman hath anointed my feet with ointment.

47. Wherefore I say unto thee, Her sins, which are many, are forgiven; for she loved much: but to whom little is forgiven, the same loveth little.

48. And he said unto her, Thy sins are forgiven.

49. And they that sat at meat with him began to say within themselves, Who is this that forgiveth sins also?

50. And he said to the woman, Thy faith hath saved thee; go in peace.

This simple story is often overlooked as a parable. It is generally thought to be an illustration used by the Lord in his discussion with Simon. But because of its parabolic form and spiritual application, I have classified it as one of the Lord's parables.

This is another parable that derives its meaning from its setting. Jesus had been invited to the home of a Pharisee whose name was Simon. The situation was not uncommon in his time.[24]

However, as Jesus came to the feast, the traditional observances and customs of hospitality to honor such a guest were not observed. Simon had not provided the common courtesies; no water had been prepared for the Lord to wash his feet and hands (Genesis 18:4); nor had the courtesy of a kiss in peace been given to him (2 Samuel 15:5); nor was oil provided for his head as was customary at such festivals (Psalm 23:5). Apparently intentionally, his host had been sadly lacking in warmth and hospitality.[25]

The houses at that time were constructed to allow easy access, and it was not uncommon to have someone enter on such an occasion to listen to the discussion, or for the poor to actually participate in the meal. It was, however, uncommon for a woman to do so.[26] A woman, unnamed in the scripture, came to the feast because she knew that Jesus was in the house.

In the scriptures the woman is designated as "a sinner."[27] This classification usually meant that she had been immoral, but nowhere is this specifically mentioned of her. She had brought with her "an alabaster box of ointment" and stood at the feet of Jesus as he was reclining in the traditional method of eating, his head and body leaning toward the table and his feet away from it.[28]

Simon observed the woman touch Jesus, and he demonstrated a "holier than thou" attitude when he thought to himself, "This man, if he were a prophet, would have known who and what manner of woman this is that toucheth him: for she is a sinner." The Jews believed that the mark of a great prophet, and certainly the Messiah, was the ability to discern spirits,[29] a belief grounded in scripture (see Isaiah 11:3–4). Simon's conclusion was that Jesus could not discern that the woman was a sinner, and thus lacked one of the qualifications of a prophet. Jesus perceived his thoughts, and countered with the parable of the two debtors as an explanation of his acceptance of the woman:

There were two debtors, one with a great debt and one with a small one. They both had the same creditor, and due to their penniless condition, the creditor forgave them of their debts. The Lord asked Simon, "Which of them will love him most?" "I suppose," Simon responded, "that he, to whom he forgave most." Jesus immediately acknowledged that this was the correct answer. Then he applied the parable to the sinful woman and Simon. Simon had offered the Savior no water but the woman had washed the Savior's feet with her tears and wiped them with her hair. Simon had given Jesus no kiss of salutation, yet the woman had not ceased to kiss his feet. Simon had provided no oil, yet she had anointed Jesus' feet with ointment. The Lord readily forgave her sins, concluding, "For she loved much: but to whom little is forgiven, the same loveth little." Simon painfully understood the application of the parable.

Several questions raised by the parable need further discussion:

First, there has been much speculation as to who the unnamed woman in this parable was. Many feel it was either Mary, the sister of Lazarus—a speculation partially derived from the fact that she had given Jesus a similar anointing (Matthew 26:6–13; Mark 14:3–9; John 12:1–8)—or Mary Magdalene. But there is no evidence to support either theory, and no such inference should be drawn.[30]

Even though it might seem unusual to have two such anointings reported in the scriptures, it seems clear from the record that such was the case. Consider the following:

A. Although offense was taken at both anointings, in Luke the offense was taken by Simon, the host, and was directed toward the Lord. The offense in the other Gospels was taken by Judas, and was directed toward Mary.

B. Although Simon is the name of the host in both instances, it is "perhaps the commonest of Jewish names."[31]

C. The reasons for the anointings are different. In Luke the woman anoints Jesus because of the love she has for the Savior and the forgiveness she is seeking. According to Jesus, Mary anoints him in token of his burial (JST John 12:7).

D. The woman in Luke is reported to be a sinner. Such sinfulness was never imputed to Mary, the sister of Lazarus.

E. The two anointings are recorded in different stages of the Lord's ministry. The Luke anointing occurred early, sometime during the Lord's Galilean ministry,[32] whereas Mary's anointing occurred during the last days of Christ's ministry. Both anointings were purposefully recorded by the Gospel writers to edify the teachings surrounding them.[33]

Second: The parable of the two debtors used the analogy of a creditor to refer to God, debtor to refer to sinners, and debts to represent sins. In the parable the larger debtor represented the woman and the smaller debtor represented Simon. When the Lord applied the parable to Simon and the woman, he indicated that she loved much, because she had been forgiven much; but that one who had been forgiven little possessed little love for God. It seems to appear from the parable that the more sins one has, the more love one is capable of. But it is more probable that the word *sinner* as used here, does not refer to the quantity of one's transgressions as much as it does to the degree of consciousness one has of his sins and his desire for forgiveness. Had Simon felt a great desire for forgiveness of his transgressions (even though they may not have been as serious or numerous as the woman's), he too would have felt great love for the Lord.

This great desire for forgiveness was produced by the woman's faith in Jesus, which he acknowledged when he forgave her (Luke 7:50). This is exactly what Simon, the proud Pharisee, lacked. He derived little or no good from his meeting with the Christ, whereas the woman, in her brief encounter, bore away the blessings of forgiveness.

Third: There is no indication that the woman in the parable had known or been taught by Jesus prior to this occasion; however, it is evident that she was deeply repentant and contrite. On a previous occasion Jesus had taught, "Come unto me, all ye that labour and are heavy laden, and I will give you rest" (Matthew 11:28), and the woman's actions indicate that perhaps she had heard this teaching either from Jesus or from others, for she seemed to come to Jesus for that specific reason.[34]

The principle of forgiveness would be taught by the Lord in other ways and at other times, but it could not have been more beautifully exemplified than by this simple parable.

Mercy

The Unmerciful Servant

Matthew 18:23–35

23. Therefore is the kingdom of heaven likened unto a certain king, which would take account of his servants.

24. And when he had begun to reckon, one was brought unto him, which owed him ten thousand talents.

25. But forasmuch as he had not to pay, his lord commanded him to be sold, and his wife, and children, and all that he had, and payment to be made.

26. The servant therefore fell down, and worshipped him, saying, Lord, have patience with me, and I will pay thee all.

27. Then the lord of that servant was moved with compassion, and loosed him, and forgave him the debt.

28. But the same servant went out, and found one of his fellowservants, which owed him an hundred pence: and he laid hands on him, and took him by the throat, saying, Pay me that thou owest.

29. And his fellowservant fell down at his feet, and besought him, saying, Have patience with me, and I will pay thee all.

30. And he would not: but went and cast him into prison, till he should pay the debt.

31. So when his fellowservants saw what was done, they were very sorry, and came and told unto their lord all that was done.

32. Then his lord, after that he had called him, said unto him, O thou wicked servant, I forgave thee all that debt, because thou desiredst me:

33. Shouldest not thou also have had compassion on thy fellowservant, even as I had pity on thee?

34. And his lord was wroth, and delivered him to the tormentors, till he should pay all that was due unto him.

35. So likewise shall my heavenly Father do also unto you, if ye from your hearts forgive not every one his brother their trespasses.

It would be impossible to derive the full impact and meaning from this parable without discussing the Lord's teachings prior to it. His Apostles had come to him asking who would be the greatest in the kingdom of heaven, and in answer to this verbal evidence of ambition, Jesus had used the example of a small child (Matthew 18:1—6) to indicate that their efforts at self-aggrandizement were not acceptable in the kingdom of God. He emphasized this with the parable of the lost sheep.[35] He then taught them concerning the second great commandment and their responsibility with regard to offenses from their fellowman (Matthew 18:15—17).

At the conclusion of these instructions, Peter continued to question the Lord about relationships, asking, "How oft shall my brother sin against me, and I forgive him?" Without waiting for an answer from the Lord he added, "till seven times?" (Matthew 18:21.) The question, with its self-proclaimed answer, might very well indicate how far Peter had already been influenced by the spirit of the Lord.[36] The Jewish masters required that the offender be forgiven only three times.[37] This requirement was grounded upon Jehovah's instructions to Amos (Amos 1:3; 2:6). Yet Peter more than doubled the legal requirement in his comment to the Lord, and he undoubtedly thought that he had caught the true spirit of the Master's teachings. But Jesus proceeded to raise Peter's limited earthly vision to the eternal heights of the kingdom of God. The apparent error in Peter's question came from the implication that in forgiving, a man gave up a right that he might under certain circumstances exercise, that is, not forgiving. It seems to be the purpose of the Lord's response to "make clear that when God calls on a member of His kingdom to forgive, He does not call on him to renounce a right, but that he has now no right to exercise in the matter; asking for and accepting forgiveness, he has implicitly pledged himself to show it."[38]

Thus the Lord responded that to forgive seven times only was not enough, but that a person should forgive "until seventy times seven" (Matthew 18:22). The answer indicated the responsibility of the righteous to forgive, not just on occasion, but at all times (D&C 64:10). At this point the Lord gave the parable of the unmerciful servant.

The parable begins with a certain king who was determined to take account of his servants. The king represents God and the servants represent his children, or man.[39] One of the servants was brought before the king to give an account of his debt. Note that he was "brought" before the king rather than coming of his own accord. Although some may report of their own accord for an accounting, others must be forced to appear. "The messengers who serve the summons may be adversity, illness, the approach of death," or some other catastrophe or calamity. Whatever the messengers' disguise, "they enforce a rendering of our accounts."[40]

The servant owed an enormous debt of ten thousand talents to the king. It was a debt so large that it was obvious the servant could never repay it.[41]

In his wrath the king commanded that the servant's wife and children and all that he had be sold in order that payment be made. This was a circumstance not unfamiliar at the time of Jesus,[42] but was parabolic dressing in the parable, pointing out man's utter hopelessness without God's forgiveness. Yet the servant pleaded his case, falling down and worshipping the king. In his prostrate position he begged the king to have patience with him, and he would repay the entire debt.

The parable portrays man as a debtor to God (Mosiah 2:23–24), a mere steward over God's abundant blessings. If we misuse those blessings or disobey the commandments, we incur an enormous debt to the Lord. Justice would require retribution and punishment.[43] However, through faith, humility, and repentance, we can, so to speak, cast ourselves at the feet of the King and invoke his infinite compassion to save us from punishment. And through adherence to the laws of repentance, we can be relieved of the debt which we have incurred.

Now the second point of the parable unfolds. The servant leaves the presence of the king and finds a fellow servant who owes him a very small amount of money (when compared to the enormous debt he has so recently been forgiven). The first servant now has the opportunity to extend toward his fellow servant the same mercy he has just received from the king.

When the first servant demands payment from his fellow servant, the fellow servant asks him to have patience and he will pay all. But the first servant ignores the great mercy recently extended to him by the king, and taking his fellow servant by the throat, drags him to the prison and casts him in until he can pay the debt.

His actions are totally incongruous with those of the king, and are placed in the parable to emphasize the moral of the parabolic story. The actions of the unmerciful servant are reported to the king, and he is again brought before him. The king reminds him of the great forgiveness and mercy that he has received, and asks him why he did not show similar compassion to his fellow servant.

The parable now draws to a conclusion. All of the previous debt that had been forgiven is now restored. Because the servant cannot pay it, he is delivered to the tormentors until he pays all that is due. But he cannot suffer enough to pay the debt, nor could he ever make amends sufficient to absolve himself from his guilt; therefore, the banishment is endless.[44]

The requirement in Peter's question of "how oft shall my brother sin against me, and I forgive him?" was not the seven times volunteered by Peter, nor the amplified seven times seventy expressed by the Lord. For the Lord, in explanation of the parable, stated, "So likewise shall my heavenly Father do also unto you, if ye from your hearts forgive not every one his brother their trespasses."

In the Sermon on the Mount the Lord had declared, "Blessed are the merciful: for they shall obtain mercy" (Matthew 5:7). He now extended the principle through this parable. If we are to expect mercy from our Father in Heaven, we are required to extend mercy to our fellowman; clearly we must forgive without retribution or vengeance, and "we must forgive even if [the] offender [does] not repent and ask forgiveness."[45]

Stephen exemplified this principle. As he was being stoned for preaching the resurrected Christ, he "kneeled down, and cried with a loud voice, Lord, lay not this sin to their charge" (Acts 7:60). As demonstrated in the parable, the first servant came under condemnation not for defaulting on his debt, but for not showing mercy to a fellow servant after the king had extended such great mercy to him. His sin was that he remained unmerciful after having received mercy.

James taught this principle in his admonitions to the Saints when he declared, "For he shall have judgment without mercy, that hath shewed no mercy" (James 2:13). Lack of mercy for our fellowman is a sin of serious proportions.[46] By sinning anew and not extending the mercy he had so readily received, the servant in the parable fell back into the darkness out of which he had been delivered. All of his previous debt (his former evils) would now add to the darkness into which he would be cast.

Paul later admonished the Colossians to put on the new (spiritual) man, "Forbearing one another, and forgiving one another, if any man have a quarrel against any: even as Christ forgave you, so also do ye" (Colossians 3:13). And to the Ephesians he declared, "And be ye kind one to another, tenderhearted, forgiving one another, even as God for Christ's sake hath forgiven you" (Ephesians 4:32). "He who will not forgive others breaks down the bridge over which he himself must travel."[47]

Those who extend to others the divine forgiveness which they have experienced characterize the true love of Christ. On one occasion the disciples asked the Savior to teach them how to pray. He responded with what is called the Lord's Prayer, which contains the phrase, "Forgive us our debts, as we forgive our debtors" (Matthew 6:12). Through the parable of the unmerciful servant the Lord taught his disciples this divine principle of mercy with unprecedented clarity.

Mercy is for the merciful.

Teaching Relationships 6

As the Lord taught the gospel he gave instructions governing the relationships between man and God, man and worldly possessions, and man and his fellowman.

The Law of Moses had been a preparatory law. All things contained therein looked forward to the coming of the Messiah and his kingdom and attempted to prepare the children of Israel for the great event. But now the Messiah had come, and a new law had been given. The old law was in process of fulfillment; the new law was capable of giving man exaltation in the kingdom of God. Man's relationship to God, to the world, and to his fellowman would no longer be rigidly prescribed, but was to flow from the depths of human love and understanding. The parables in this chapter teach these relationships.

Man to God

The Unprofitable Servants

Luke 17:7—10

7. But which of you, having a servant plowing or feeding cattle, will say unto him by and by, when he is

come from the field, Go and sit down to meat?

8. And will not rather say unto him, Make ready wherewith I may sup, and gird thyself, and serve me, till I have eaten and drunken; and afterward thou shalt eat and drink?

9. Doth he thank that servant because he did the things that were commanded him? I trow not.

10. So likewise ye, when ye shall have done all those things which are commanded you, say, We are unprofitable servants: we have done that which was our duty to do.

This parable is not uniformly treated as a parable by all writers, and perhaps could be referred to as a parabolic sermon.[1] The Lord used this parable as an analogy in his instructions to his disciples when he admonished them to be diligent and full of unselfish devotion, tolerance, and forgiveness.[2] As he concludes, his disciples request of him, "Lord, increase our faith." It was not that they did not have faith in God and in Jesus as the Messiah, but they wanted enlightenment. They had heard his admonitions of godliness; now they wanted Jesus to elaborate on their relationship with their Father in Heaven. In this parable the Lord compared the Apostles and God to a servant and his master. The parable may have reflected the incorrect religious beliefs of the day, that is, that rewards received were in direct proportion to exactness in work and obedience to the Law.[3]

In this parable the master had a servant who had worked all day. The servant did not expect, immediately upon completion of his work, to eat and rest. When he finished his normal work, he was required to do more. He must first serve the master his supper before he himself could eat. The servant was not thanked by the master, for it was his duty to do that which he was commanded to do—that was his obligation as a servant. He was obligated to do his duty, and the master had the right to demand it of him. The servant could not even demand compensation for his services.[4] The estimate of his worth was solely the responsibility of the master. The Lord was trying to teach his disciples that the quality of their faith would be gauged by their obedience and untiring service to the master.[5]

When the servant had done all of the things that he had been commanded to do, he was yet accounted as an unprofitable servant, for he had done only that which he was required to do.[6]

King Benjamin, in his final address to the people, enumerated clearly the principle taught in this parable when he declared:

> I say unto you, my brethren, that if you should render all the thanks and praise which your whole soul has power to possess, to that God who has created you, and has kept and preserved you, and has caused that ye should rejoice, and has granted that ye should live in peace one with another—I say unto you that if ye should serve him who has created you from the beginning, and is preserving you from day to day, by lending you breath, that ye may live and move and do according to your own will, and even supporting you from one moment to another—I say, if ye should serve him with all your whole souls yet ye would be unprofitable servants. (Mosiah 2:20–21).

The Savior's instruction left the Apostles with a clear understanding of their relationship to him and his Father. Their obligation as disciples and Apostles was as the servant to the master. They were expected to do their duty without concern for compensation; this was to be their simple and earnest faith. Faith was to be the seed planted and nourished until it sprouted and began to grow; it was not to have a perfect knowledge of things, but was the substance of things hoped for and the evidence of things not seen (Alma 32:21–30; Hebrews 11:1).

The Apostles were to give no offense and take no offense from the Master. God was their master, and would continually support them, granting them all that they needed in order to perform the duty which they, as servants, were obligated to perform. Still they would be accounted unprofitable servants, "still indebted unto him . . . and will be, forever and ever" (Mosiah 2:24). God's gifts to his people are far greater than they will ever be capable of repaying.

To Worldly Treasures

The Unjust Steward

Luke 16:1–9

1. And he said also unto his disciples, There was a certain rich man, which had a steward; and the same was

accused unto him that he
had wasted his goods.
2. And he called him,
and said unto him, How is it
that I hear this of thee? give
an account of thy stewardship; for thou mayest be no
longer steward.
3. Then the steward said
within himself, What shall I
do? for my lord taketh away
from me the stewardship: I
cannot dig; to beg I am
ashamed.
4. I am resolved what to
do, that, when I am put out
of the stewardship, they
may receive me into their
houses.
5. So he called every one
of his lord's debtors unto
him, and said unto the first,
How much owest thou unto
my lord?
6. And he said, An hun-
dred measures of oil. And he
said unto him, Take thy bill,
and sit down quickly, and
write fifty.
7. Then said he to
another, And how much
owest thou? And he said,
An hundred measures of
wheat. And he said unto
him, Take thy bill, and write
fourscore.
8. And the lord com-
mended the unjust steward,
because he had done wisely:
for the children of this world
are in their generation wiser
than the children of light.
9. And I say unto you,
Make to yourselves friends
of the mammon of unrigh-
teousness; that, when ye fail,
they may receive you into
everlasting habitations.

All of the parables in the sixteenth chapter of Luke are recorded only by Luke. They contain a common philosophy involving the debilitating effect of the things of the world (or those things highly esteemed by man) upon the spiritual requirements of the kingdom of heaven. Luke's Gospel is heavily laden with this emphasis.[7] "The love of money had become a characteristic of [the] decaying religiousness" of the Pharisees and the rulers of the Jews, even to the extent that the rich should use their wealth "to make friends for the future world, instead of enjoying it here."[8] This teaching would have been known to the Apostles, and it seems that, to some degree, they believed it. The story of the rich young ruler and Christ's instructions to him, as well as the questions the Apostles posed afterward, seems to confirm this.

The rich young ruler came to Jesus before his final entry into Jerusalem and asked, "What shall I do to inherit eternal life?" (Luke 18:18.) It was not an unusual question,[9] and Jesus answered it by enumerating several commandments. To this the man responded that he had kept all of these commandments from his youth. Jesus accepted this answer, but desired that the young man should proceed beyond the Law of Moses. So he commanded him to sell all that he had, distribute it to the poor, and follow Him. The young man received these instructions sorrowfully, for he was very rich, and he would not comply with the Lord's request. Acknowledging the young man's problems, Jesus commented, "For it is easier for a camel to go through a needle's eye, than for a rich man to enter into the kingdom of God" (Luke 18:25).

The Apostles had heard all that was said. They were astonished at the Lord's comment and the relationship that he had drawn between the possession of the things of the world and the attainment of spiritual position. After the Lord had concluded his instructions they asked, "Who then can be saved?" (Luke 18:26.)

The relationship between worldly wealth and heavenly blessings, so distinctly taught in the rich ruler discourse, had been earlier expressed by the parable of the unjust steward and the instructions surrounding it. This parable dealt with man's relationship to worldly wealth, and was given to help mankind so manage "the affairs and interests and possessions of this life as not to lose hereafter their heritage of the eternal riches."[10] And now to the parable.

A rich man had a steward whom he accused of wasting his goods. The rich man called the steward before him and required him to give an account of his stewardship, and informed him that he would no longer be his steward.

The steward, knowing that he would soon lose his stewardship, determined that he must provide for himself and for his future. He decided to do this by further dissipating the goods of the master so that those to whom he gave the boon would be indebted to him in the things of the world and would therefore "receive [him] into their houses." He called in first one debtor and then another and reduced the amount they owed the rich man, again unjustly dissipating the goods of the master. Then the Lord made what appears to be an unusual comment: "And the Lord commended the unjust steward, because he had done wisely: for the children of this world are in their generation wiser than the children of light."

All of the salient points of the parable support this statement as the moral of the story.[11] Unless this moral is clearly understood, confusion might easily arise as to why the Lord would commend what appears to be an unethical and dishonest activity. The steward was accused of wasting the master's goods, and apparently was guilty of this misdeed, for he made no attempt to defend himself.[12] As a steward he had authority to act as he did, yet his actions were totally unrighteous.

After being caught misusing his master's goods, the steward made no attempt at repentance; he only showed fear and concern over the potential poverty and ruin that would come upon him. He determined that he would continue in his works of unrighteousness in order to secure his worldly existence.

The commending of the unjust steward is the turning point of the parable and the point at which the Lord commenced speaking. He complimented the steward for his prudence and foresight in preserving his worldly existence.[13] In the same breath, he chastised the children of light (or the saints of God) for not being as prudent as the unjust steward in preserving their spiritual rewards.[14] He proposed that the saints imitate the steward's prudence. He declared with forthrightness and clarity that the saints of God are "in the same position as this steward who saw the eminent disaster . . . but the crisis which threatens [them], in which, indeed, [they] are already involved is incomparably more terrible."[15] The unjust steward recognized his circumstance and boldly took action to preserve himself. That he incorrectly chose the things of the world over the things of eternity is obvious, but given that choice, his actions to preserve himself were commendable.

The Lord emphasized the point he was trying to make when he stated: "He that is faithful in that which is least is faithful also in much: and he that is unjust in the least is unjust also in much. If therefore ye have not been faithful in the unrighteous mammon, who will commit to your trust the true riches? And if ye have not been faithful in that which was another man's, who shall give you that which is your own? No servant can serve two masters." (Luke 16:10—13.) The things of the world often create opposition to the things of God. Using wealth unwisely can cause us to forfeit eternal riches, whereas wealth put to good purposes can increase our eternal rewards.

Worldly possessions are governed by one of two masters. One is mammon: Herein man can choose to invest his time in earthly gratifications and yield to the sensual temptations of unrighteousness. The other is God: This Master requires man to place the things of the world in proper perspective with eternal requirements, using earthly possessions in such a manner as to glorify God and lay up eternal treasures in heaven.[16]

The reaction of the Pharisees who heard the parable of the unjust steward indicates that they understood it clearly, for they "derided him" (Luke 16:14). Jesus immediately chastised them for being "in their generation" the children of "this world," and said, "Ye are they which justify yourselves before men; but God knoweth your hearts: for that which is highly esteemed among men is abomination in the sight of God" (Luke 16:15).

Thus ended one of the most unusual of the Lord's parables, the only one in which a negative statement taught the positive things of God. However, the conclusion of the parable is clear. Things of the world, highly esteemed by man, have little value to God.

To gain exaltation in the kingdom of heaven, the things of the world (the mammon of unrighteousness) must be subordinated to the things of God. Man should "emulate the unjust steward and the lovers of mammon, not in their dishonesty, cupidity, and miserly hoarding of the wealth that is at best transitory, but in their zeal, forethought, and provision for the future."[17]

The things of the world are not to become our master, but our servant.

To Fellowman

The Wedding Guests

Luke 14:7–11

7. And he put forth a parable to those which were bidden, when he marked how they chose out the chief rooms; saying unto them,

8. When thou art bidden

of any man to a wedding, sit not down in the highest room; lest a more honourable man than thou be bidden of him;

9. And he that bade thee and him come and say to thee, Give this man place; and thou begin with shame to take the lowest room.

10. But when thou art bidden, go and sit down in the lowest room; that when he that bade thee cometh, he may say unto thee, Friend, go up higher: then shalt thou have worship in the presence of them that sit at meat with thee.

11. For whosoever exalteth himself shall be abased; and he that humbleth himself shall be exalted.

The setting of this parable is similar to that of the two debtors.[18] Jesus had been invited to the home of one of the chief Pharisees to partake of the Sabbath meal. The Sabbath at Jesus' time was a day used by the rabbis for social entertainment.[19] The invitation was not abnormal, but those who extended it in this case had sinister intentions. Luke reports that they "watched him" (Luke 14:1), and it appears that the sole purpose of the invitation was to lure him to do evil in their eyes. (It was at this dinner that the miracle of the man with the dropsy was performed.)[20]

As was the tradition at the time, the places at the table were assigned according to the reputation and social status of those in attendance—the most "important" guests receiving the best positions. The customs of the Pharisees had deteriorated to the point that they were totally self-aggrandizing, even in their hospitality.[21] Jesus used their customs to instruct the Pharisees in humility. "Sit not down in the highest room," he admonished them, lest you have to give up your seat and become ashamed because a more honorable man than you should come to the gathering. But "when thou art bidden, go and sit down in the lowest room" that the host may bid you to a higher position, and "then shalt thou have worship in the presence of them that sit at meat with thee." Serve your fellowmen, he taught, and wait for your recompense to be made by God "at the resurrection of the just" (Luke 14:14).

Christ's teachings were breathing new life into the customs and traditions of the Jews[22] as he taught them of the second great commandment: Love your fellowman.

The Second Great Commandment 7

There is no doubt that Israel clearly understood the first great commandment: "Thou shalt love the Lord thy God with all thy heart, and with all thy soul, and with all thy strength, and with all thy mind" (Luke 10:27). The second great commandment was like unto it: "Thou shalt love thy neighbour as thyself" (Matthew 22:39). But this commandment lacked the emphasis and definition of the first commandment.

Whereas the Law of Moses was centered on the first commandment, the gospel of Christ recognizes that the two commandments are completely interrelated. How man loves and treats his fellowman determines how he loves his God. Jesus taught, "Inasmuch as ye have done it unto one of the least of these my brethren, ye have done it unto me," and, "Inasmuch as ye did it not to one of the least of these, ye did it not to me" (Matthew 25:40, 45). On these two laws rested all the law and the prophets.

The following parable, the good Samaritan, beautifully teaches the principles encompassed within the second great commandment.

The Good Samaritan

Luke 10:30–37

30. And Jesus answering said, A certain man went down from Jerusalem to Jericho, and fell among thieves, which stripped him of his raiment, and wounded him, and departed, leaving him half dead.

31. And by chance there came down a certain priest that way: and when he saw him, he passed by on the other side.

32. And likewise a Levite, when he was at the place, came and looked on him, and passed by on the other side.

33. But a certain Samaritan, as he journeyed, came where he was: and when he saw him, he had compassion on him,

34. And went to him, and bound up his wounds, pouring in oil and wine, and set him on his own beast, and brought him to an inn, and took care of him.

35. And on the morrow when he departed, he took out two pence, and gave them to the host, and said unto him, Take care of him; and whatsoever thou spendest more, when I come again, I will repay thee.

36. Which now of these three, thinkest thou, was neighbor unto him that fell among the thieves?

37. And he said, He that shewed mercy on him. Then said Jesus unto him, Go, and do thou likewise.

A lawyer stood before Jesus and, as Luke reports, "tempted him," by posing a question. The use of the words *tempted him* might lead some to assume that the question was posed to the Savior for some evil intent. Although this may have been the case on other occasions, it was not necessarily so in this instance. Though he may have wished to test the well-known teacher, possibly even to embarrass him, there does not appear to have been any malicious intent on the part of the lawyer[1] when he asked, "What shall I do to inherit eternal life?" (Luke 10:25.)[2]

The lawyer was, in all probability, an expert in Jewish canon law and, knowing the habits of his class, that it was common to test or try great rabbis in the rabbinical writings, he asked the question so as to involve Jesus in dialectic difficulties and subtle disputations. "Indeed, this was part of Rabbinism, and led to that painful and fatal trifling with truth, when everything became [a] matter of dialectic subtlety, and nothing was really sacred."[3]

Jesus responded to the lawyer's question with a question of his own. "What is written in the law? how readest thou?" (Luke 10:26.) The lawyer answered by reciting the first great commandment: "Love the Lord thy God with all thy heart, and with all thy soul, and with all thy strength, and with all thy mind" (Luke 10:27; Deuteronomy 6:5). To this he added the second great commandment, "and thy neighbour as thyself," since this was also required under the Levitical law (Leviticus 19:18). Jesus readily acknowledged the accuracy of the response and continued, "This do, and thou shalt live" (Luke 10:28).

Had the discussion between the lawyer and the Lord ended with this admonition, the parable would not have been given. But the lawyer continued the discussion in an attempt to "justify himself," and asked Jesus, "Who is my neighbour?" (Luke 10:29.) This question gives additional credence to the theory that the lawyer had engaged Jesus in conversation without malice or evil intent, and only for the purpose of displaying dialectical skills. By asking the second question he sought to vindicate himself from the first, and demonstrate to Jesus that the subject was not quite so easily settled as Jesus' answer implied.[4]

God had long since separated the people of Israel unto himself, and had sought to purify them that they would be holy and sanctified before him. As a result, the question "who is my neighbour?" frequently engaged the rabbis and the answer was only too clear. To the Jews, their neighbor was indeed another Jew, or member of the house of Israel.[5]

The principle involved in the question "who is my neighbour?" is very similar to that posed by Peter, when he asked the Lord how many times he should forgive his brother (Matthew 18:21–22). Jewish law dictated that the requirement was to forgive your brother three times. Both Peter and the lawyer asked their questions to determine the *limitations* of the Law and to explicitly define their responsibility under it. But the second great commandment could not be restricted in this manner.

While the lawyer sought a definite limitation on who his neighbor was, the fact remained that no boundary existed.[6]

The Lord gave the parable of the good Samaritan to enlighten his questioners as well as all those who heard his voice. He was trying to show the people how far the Law had gone astray from its original purpose, for the parable portrayed not an enlargement of the Law, as understood by the chosen people of his day, but a change in it.[7] Those who would follow the Master would no longer be bound by duty, but by love. And there was no limitation as to whom this love should be given: It was to be given freely to all mankind. To this extent the parable was a rebuke to the second question proposed by the lawyer, with its legal ramifications and nuances inferred from the Rabbinical Law. Once again Jesus did not directly answer the question, but instead gave the following parable.

A certain man went down from Jerusalem to Jericho and fell among thieves and was wounded and left for dead. The setting of the parable is purely local and Jewish in nature.[8] A man had been following the solitary desert road between Jerusalem and Jericho, "a district notoriously insecure,"[9] and had been attacked and injured.

A priest and then a Levite came upon the man as they traveled the same eighteen- to twenty-one-mile stretch of road. They viewed his plight, but passed by on the other side. Both should have assisted the injured traveler, but the intention of the parable was to depict how far astray the Mosaic Law had gone and how little the Jews understood the second great commandment. Both men may have justified their actions. The priest might have assumed that the man was dead; to come in contact with the dead under the Levitical Law was to become unclean, and so he passed by. However, the Levite "looked on him" and knew that he was not dead, yet he also passed by, perhaps fearing that the robbers were still in the vicinity or that the man was pretending to be injured in order to ensnare unsuspecting travelers. However they salved their consciences, the parable exemplified the selfish nature of Judaism common at the time of Jesus.

Finally, a Samaritan came upon the injured man. Jesus undoubtedly chose a Samaritan to show compassion because the race was severely hated by the Jews. To have a Samaritan be the one who stopped to help the injured man would have been completely unexpected and would have mortified and humbled the Lord's Jewish audience.[10] The Lord described, with minute detail, the compassion and love of the Samaritan as he developed the last part of the parable:

The Samaritan first cleansed the injured man's wounds with wine and then poured oil into them to soothe the pain. This was the costliest of remedies, but was highly esteemed in the East.[11] He then bound the wounds and took the injured man to an inn, cared for him throughout the balance of the day and night, and as he departed, left two pence to ensure that the care would continue. Then he went the extra mile and left instructions with the innkeeper to continue treatment until the man was healed, and if it cost more than two pence, he would pay the innkeeper when he returned.

The lawyer had asked Jesus, "Who is my neighbour?" Now Jesus countered that question and said, "Which now of these three, thinkest thou, was neighbour unto him that fell among the thieves?" The Lord had changed the lawyer's question from "who is my neighbour" to *"whose neighbor am I?"*

The lawyer had asked his question from a stilted, narrow, and unloving perspective. The Lord's response appealed to a far greater principle than that in which the lawyer had been trained. The Lord's question made the lawyer aware of the great gulf that existed between his knowledge of the Law and his actions under it.[12]

To the one learned in the Law, the intent of the parable was now plain, and the lawyer saw only one possible response to the question. Although it humbled him to acknowledge it, and unable to even speak the word *Samaritan,* he answered, "He that shewed mercy on him." The Lord responded succinctly, "Go, and do thou likewise." The lawyer had answered his own question and had been clearly instructed in his duty. Never again could he use the technical legalities of the old Law to justify inaction and discrimination, for the Messiah had declared that it is the responsibility of everyone to become a neighbor to all by serving those who are in need.[13]

Part Four

Teaching Accountability and Reward

Parables That Teach Accountability and Reward 8

Responsibility was fundamental to Christ's new gospel. Under its provisions there would be no more competition between individuals to achieve promised rewards. No longer was it vital to seek out the chief seats in the synagogue or uppermost rooms at feasts (Matthew 23:6). Nor was it important to receive public salutations, to be called Rabbi, or to enlarge phylacteries and the borders of garments to be seen of men (Matthew 23:5; Mark 12:38). The Savior's disciples were expected to excel—to be better than before—but not as compared with someone else. Competition was to be against oneself. In the future, each person would be responsible for what he had been given and what he did with it. Each possessed different talents and different abilities, but all had been given something. The Lord gave us the requirements for achieving his kingdom, and he will judge how well we fulfill them.

The Talents

Matthew 25:14–30

14. For the kingdom of heaven is as a man travelling into a far country, who called his own servants, and

delivered unto them his goods.

15. And unto one he gave five talents, to another two, and to another one; to every man according to his several ability; and straightway took his journey.

16. Then he that had received the five talents went and traded with the same, and made them other five talents.

17. And likewise he that had received two, he also gained other two.

18. But he that had received one went and digged in the earth, and hid his lord's money.

19. After a long time the lord of those servants cometh, and reckoneth with them.

20. And so he that had received five talents came and brought other five talents, saying, Lord, thou deliveredst unto me five talents: behold, I have gained beside them five talents more.

21. His lord said unto him, Well done, thou good and faithful servant: thou hast been faithful over a few things, I will make thee ruler over many things: enter thou into the joy of thy lord.

22. He also that had received two talents came and said, Lord, thou deliveredst unto me two talents: behold, I have gained two other talents beside them.

23. His lord said unto him, Well done, good and faithful servant; thou hast been faithful over a few things, I will make thee ruler over many things: enter thou into the joy of thy lord.

24. Then he which had received the one talent came and said, Lord, I knew thee that thou art an hard man, reaping where thou hast not sown, and gathering where thou hast not strawed:

25. And I was afraid, and went and hid thy talent in the earth: lo, there thou hast that is thine.

26. His lord answered and said unto him, Thou wicked and slothful servant, thou knewest that I reap where I sowed not, and gather where I have not strawed:

27. Thou oughtest therefore to have put my money to the exchangers, and then at my coming I should have received mine own with usury.

28. Take therefore the talent from him, and give it unto him which hath ten talents.

29. For unto every one that hath shall be given, and

he shall have abundance: but from him that hath not shall be taken away even that which he hath.

30. And cast ye the unprofitable servant into outer darkness: there shall be weeping and gnashing of teeth.

This parable was given to the Apostles in private during the last days Jesus served with them, and just before his betrayal and crucifixion. It was first interpreted by the primitive church in the Christological sense (which applied it directly to the second coming of Christ).[1] However, it should be interpreted in conjunction with the other teachings of Jesus concerning accountability and reward.[2] It was given to arouse the Apostles and the people to a realization of the significance of their daily actions, rather than to make them anticipate the Second Coming and the Judgment as the only time they would be called to account.

The application of the parable might be directly compared to Nephi's admonition concerning our laxity in this life when he envisaged people saying, "Eat, drink, and be merry, for tomorrow we die; and it shall be well with us," and said of Satan, "Others will he pacify, and lull them away into carnal security, that they will say: All is well in Zion; yea, Zion prospereth, all is well" (2 Nephi 28:7, 21). It is necessary to recognize that not all judgments take place at the second coming of Christ or at the final judgment. Man can be called to account at any moment, as graphically depicted in the parable of the foolish rich man.[3] In addition, Amulek declared that this life was the day given to us to prepare for eternity, and warned us against procrastinating the day of our repentance until we are brought to that awful crisis. Amulek then said, "If ye have procrastinated the day of your repentance even until death, behold, ye have become subjected to the spirit of the devil, and . . . the Spirit of the Lord hath withdrawn from you" (Alma 34:35).

Therefore, the parable of the talents warns each person of the impending accounting he will be required to make and the potential reward that will be given (regardless of the time that these will take place). Although specifically given to the Apostles, this parable can be applied to all those who receive entrusted gifts from God.[4] It is not limited to spiritual gifts, but can apply to all that man has been given and that he has the power to acquire through his abilities, whether these gifts be mental or physical. Any and all of the endowments that man has been given come from God and are to be used for spiritual purposes. For it is God "who has created you from the beginning, and is preserving you from day to day, by lending you breath . . . and even supporting you from one moment to another" (Mosiah 2:21).

The main theme of the parable deals with how God-given gifts should be used. It intimates that where much is given, much is required (Luke 12:48; D&C 82:3). As the Lord tells the story of the talents, certain scenes come to mind:

First Scene: The Stewardship.

The Lord tells the story about a man who was going to travel into a far country. He would be gone for some time; therefore, he entrusted his goods to the care of his servants. The inference is that they were to use the goods in his behalf while he was gone, and not just hold them in safekeeping.

He gave one servant five talents; another, two; and a third, one. Each had been given according to their ability to use the talents they received. The master left, fully expecting an increase on his goods when he returned.

The parable was deliberately couched in this manner. The servant that received two talents might not have been able to successfully handle five, and the servant receiving one might not have been able to handle two. However, the parable assumed that they could all handle that which they had received.[5]

In spite of the varying number of talents entrusted to the servants, their ability to labor was equal. They were equally capable of using the talents they had received for and in behalf of the master.[6]

Second Scene: The Accounting.

The master was gone "a long time," but eventually he returned and reckoned with the servants to determine how they had used their talents. Those who had received five and two talents, respectively, stepped forward boldly to declare their gain for and in behalf of the master. They had been diligent in their application of the talents and although they had been entrusted with diverse amounts, they each had an increase to present to the master—each had doubled the amount left with him. To this the master gave his wholehearted congratulations. He commended the faithful servants, promising them that they would be made rulers over many things and inviting them to "enter . . . into the joy of thy lord."

Now the servant who had received but one talent stepped forward and presented his talent to the Lord. He had been afraid of the responsibility he had been given, and had been idle and unwilling to work. His excuses are indicative of his mendacious attitude, and his grumbling answer to the master even implied that his master had been unrighteous.[7] He had not used his talent at all, but had dug into the earth and hidden it.

This imagery depicts a slothful and unwise servant (D&C 58:26–29). He had performed no labor, shown no devotion, and exemplified no faithfulness in the use of his talent. He had completely wasted his opportunity.[8] His failure to use the gift fulfilled Moroni's statement that if the day should ever come "that the power and gifts of God shall be done away among you, it shall be because of unbelief" (Moroni 10:24).

With this imagery, the Lord emphasized the complete negligence of the inept servant. The man was deceiving himself, for in his heart he attributed to the Lord the slothful traits that he himself possessed.[9] He had not even performed that which was considered to be the least he could have done, for the Lord pointed out that he could have placed the money with "the exchangers," so that when he returned he could have received something for the talent he had entrusted to the servant.

Final Scene: The Reward.

The servants who had done well for the Lord received his grace and were granted the promise of a future reward, entrance into God's kingdom. All who are diligent in the righteous use of their talents can anticipate receiving the same reward, whether their talents be of a spiritual, mental, moral, or physical nature.[10]

Then the Lord turned his attention to the third servant. His talent was taken away from him. It cannot be said that this action was unfair; rather it was a natural and normal consequence of the servant's actions.

An example of just such an occurrence appears in the Old Testament. The children of Israel had been led by judges and prophets since leaving Egypt, but now they demanded that

Samuel find them a king, for they refused to accept the Lord as their King (1 Samuel 8:6–7). They specifically requested of Samuel that a king be given to them that he might "judge us like all the nations" (1 Samuel 8:5). The Lord obliged the Israelites, and Samuel called Saul to lead them.

Saul accepted the kingship, but he did not act in conformity with the requirements placed upon him by the Lord. He acted as the servant had with his talent. He did not obey with faithfulness, and in spite of his fear of the Lord, he rejected His counsel. Samuel then evoked the judgment of the Lord upon Saul, just as the Lord in the parable evoked his judgment upon the servant. "For thou hast rejected the word of the Lord, and the Lord hath rejected thee from being king over Israel" (1 Samuel 15:26). In the parable of the talents, the Lord took from the servant the single talent with which he had been entrusted. In the example of Saul Samuel said, "The Lord hath rent the kingdom of Israel from thee this day" (1 Samuel 15:28), and He gave the kingdom to another.

After the Lord took the talent from his faithless servant, he gave it to the one who had ten talents. Although some have thought this inappropriate, it follows the natural sequence of the parable. The one who had received five talents and had labored diligently and faithfully to gain five more had demonstrated his ability to use the greater gift. So from the servant who did not perform was taken even that which he had been given, and his judgment was decided: As an "unprofitable servant," he was cast into outer darkness.

This principle is in total conformity with modern revelation. The Lord revealed to Joseph Smith:

> It is not meet that I should command in all things; for he that is compelled in all things, the same is slothful and not a wise servant; wherefore he receiveth no reward.
>
> Verily I say, men should be anxiously engaged in a good cause, and do many things of their own free will, and bring to pass much righteousness;
>
> For the power is in them, wherein they are agents unto themselves. And inasmuch as men do good they shall in nowise lose their reward.
>
> But he that doeth not anything until he is commanded, and receiveth a commandment with doubtful heart, and

keepeth it with slothfulness, the same is damned." (D&C 58:26–29.)

In the parable, the talents were bestowed upon each servant in accordance with his ability to successfully use them. So, also, are we apportioned a varying number of talents. Each may not have the same number or quality of talents, but we all have at least one. We are commanded to use our talents for and in behalf of the kingdom of God. We have the agency to choose how we will use them, but if we are to achieve the kingdom, we must use them as we have been commanded by the Lord. For those who do so the promise is clear—the reward will be granted. If we do nothing, or waste the talent we have, the Lord considers us slothful and unprofitable servants, and our talents will be taken from us.[11] "Every good and faithful servant of Christ must, whatever his circumstances, personally and directly use such talent as he may have to make gain for Christ."[12]

The Pounds

Luke 19:11–27

11. And as they heard these things, he added and spake a parable, because he was nigh to Jerusalem, and because they thought that the kingdom of God should immediately appear.

12. He said therefore, A certain nobleman went into a far country to receive for himself a kingdom, and to return.

13. And he called his ten servants, and delivered them ten pounds, and said unto them, Occupy till I come.

14. But his citizens hated him, and sent a message after him, saying, We will not have this man to reign over us.

15. And it came to pass, that when he was returned, having received the kingdom, then he commanded these servants to be called unto him, to whom he had given the money, that he might know how much every man had gained by trading.

16. Then came the first, saying, Lord, thy pound hath gained ten pounds.

17. And he said unto him, Well, thou good servant: because thou hast been faithful in a very little,

have thou authority over ten cities.

18. And the second came, saying, Lord, thy pound hath gained five pounds.

19. And he said likewise to him, Be thou also over five cities.

20. And another came, saying, Lord, behold, here is thy pound, which I have kept laid up in a napkin:

21. For I feared thee, because thou art an austere man: thou takest up that thou layedst not down, and reapest that thou didst not sow.

22. And he saith unto him, Out of thine own mouth will I judge thee, thou wicked servant. Thou knewest that I was an austere man, taking up that I laid not down, and reaping that I did not sow:

23. Wherefore then gavest not thou my money into the bank, that at my coming I might have required mine own with usury?

24. And he said unto them that stood by, Take from him the pound, and give it to him that hath ten pounds.

25. (And they said unto him, Lord, he hath ten pounds.)

26. For I say unto you, That unto every one which hath shall be given; and from him that hath not, even that he hath shall be taken away from him.

27. But those mine enemies, which would not that I should reign over them, bring hither, and slay them before me.

Although similar to the parable of the talents, the parable of the pounds cannot be assumed to be merely a duplication of it, for such is not the case. A comparison of the two quickly establishes the points of difference between them.

POUNDS	TALENTS
• nobleman, not commoner	• unidentified wealthy man (indicates private citizen)
• nobleman leaves to claim kingdom	• man leaves, reason unknown
• ten entrusted servants	• three entrusted servants
• servants given same amount *regardless* of ability	• servants given varied amounts *according* to ability

• citizens of the kingdom hated nobleman	• no mistrust indicated
• example drawn from political life	• example from social life[13]
• accountability demanded at return	• accountability demanded at return
• successful servants rewarded	• successful rewarded
• extra gain varies according to success and ability	• extra gain equals success and ability
• pound taken from slothful servant	• talent taken from slothful servant
• enemies punished and destroyed	• no such occurrence

From these differences additional doctrine can be gleaned pertaining to the accountability and reward expected by those upon the earth. At one time or another, we all must come to judgment, at which time we are held accountable for the stewardship given us while we were on the earth.

The pounds, as the talents, represent the gifts of God, or the stewardship he has given us. The distinctive feature of this parable is that each servant is given the same amount (one pound) to do the best he can with in behalf of the absent nobleman. The gain is to be given to the nobleman upon his return. The injection of hatred by the citizens and their attempt to block the nobleman from receiving his kingdom is one of the more interesting facets of the parable. It perhaps reflects the recorded instance of Archelaus when he left the area of Judea for Rome. Through inheritance, he was to be endowed with a kingdom from Caesar, and the people strongly objected to that inheritance.[14]

Because this parable has a definite political involvement it must first, of necessity, be specifically applied to the Jews of Christ's day. It reflects how they viewed the Messiah and the Law under which they awaited him—but its meaning can also be projected into modern times.

The Jewish leaders believed that their meticulous observance of the Law would assure them a place in the kingdom of heaven. The Israelite nation as a whole had developed a philosophy of selfish exclusiveness based on this belief. This policy was in direct opposition to the gospel principle that the kingdom of heaven must be spread throughout the world and encompass all mankind. The Jews anticipated a political Messiah and an immediate establishment of an earthly kingdom. It would appear from the comment of Jesus as he introduced this parable that "they thought that the kingdom of God should immediately appear." Even the disciples anticipated that the establishment of the final kingdom of God would not be long in coming. But that was not the case, and the parable was given to clarify that point, and to firmly establish the fact that the servants (or mankind) must continually abide in faithfulness and devotion to the Lord in order to receive their reward.[15] If we become slack and negligent in the application of our gifts within the kingdom, our reward will be taken from us.

A division of goods occurred in this parable as in the parable of the talents, but the unique feature here is that each recipient received the same quantity: one pound. There was no consideration of ability, but "success would imply greater ability, even as it would require more constant labour."[16] The servants attained differing degrees of success in their use of the gifts and were rewarded accordingly. Unlike the talents, which were given in consideration of the servants' capabilities, the pounds multiplied according to the industry of each individual servant.

As with the parable of the talents, the story of the pounds revolves around the one servant who did nothing with the pound that he had been given. He attempted to return it unused to the nobleman, hoping still to gain his reward, and he held the same austere view of God and misapplication of the principles of the kingdom as did the servant in the parable of the talents.

He refused to do the minimum that was required of him to insure that something would be returned to the nobleman. In accordance with the requirements of the kingdom, the pound was taken from him and given to another. The parable sharply emphasized the fact that one cannot be selfishly exclusive with his gift; he must actively expand his talents if he is to acquire the kingdom of God.

The entrusted servants in this parable represented the members of the kingdom at the time of Christ. They thought that during their lifetime they would usher in the kingdom, and that their responsibility was only to prepare themselves for that event. They gave little credence to the requirement that they must actively use their gifts to prepare the world for the coming of Jesus Christ.[17] The pound was taken from the slothful servant and given to the one who had brought the greatest increase to his king—those who work the hardest receive the greatest reward.[18]

The last part of the parable talks of the citizens who rejected the nobleman and did not want him to rule over them. They were representative of the Jewish rulers of the chosen people.[19] During the trial of Jesus, Pilate would bring the Lord before them and state, "Behold your King!" (John 19:14.) Their response would be similar to that of the citizens in the parable, for they cried, "Away with him, away with him, crucify him. Pilate saith unto them, Shall I crucify your King? The chief priests answered, We have no king but Caesar." (John 19:15.)

This open and willful rejection of the Messiah was explicitly predicted in the parable of the pounds. The Jews would not have Jesus be their king, and they actively attempted to destroy his kingdom. Their reward was parabolically predicted, for the parable stated that the Lord would destroy the wicked and rebellious citizens, and they would receive no kingdom.[20]

This parable is very straightforward. The king, or nobleman, represents Christ.[21] The various uses of the pounds represent the different ways man can successfully use the gifts he has been given. A reward was granted according to the degree that the servants applied their gifts. The slothful servant was punished for his refusal to work at all,[22] a warning to lazy and fearful men and women of all ages. And finally, the citizens represent those who reject the Lord and attempt to destroy his kingdom.[23]

A final application of this parable can be made both to the Jews of Christ's time and to his Apostles, who, although anxiously involved in his work, had the mistaken idea that his political kingdom would soon be established.[24] He cautioned these beloved brethren and explained to them that they would assuredly be called upon to account for their stewardship, and that their reward would be based on the application of that stewardship toward the growth and glory of the kingdom of God.

The Labourers in the Vineyard

Matthew 20:1–16

1. For the kingdom of heaven is like unto a man that is an householder, which went out early in the morning to hire labourers into his vineyard.

2. And when he had agreed with the labourers for a penny a day, he sent them into his vineyard.

3. And he went out about the third hour, and saw others standing idle in the marketplace,

4. And said unto them; Go ye also into the vineyard, and whatsoever is right I will give you. And they went their way.

5. Again he went out about the sixth and ninth hour, and did likewise.

6. And about the eleventh hour he went out, and found others standing idle, and saith unto them, Why stand ye here all the day idle?

7. They say unto him, Because no man hath hired us. He saith unto them, Go ye also into the vineyard; and whatsoever is right, that shall ye receive.

8. So when even was come, the lord of the vineyard saith unto his steward, Call the labourers, and give them their hire, beginning from the last unto the first.

9. And when they came that were hired about the eleventh hour, they received every man a penny.

10. But when the first came, they supposed that they should have received more; and they likewise received every man a penny.

11. And when they had received it, they murmured against the goodman of the house,

12. Saying, These last have wrought but one hour, and thou hast made them equal unto us, which have borne the burden and heat of the day.

13. But he answered one of them, and said, Friend, I do thee no wrong: didst not thou agree with me for a penny?

14. Take that thine is, and go thy way: I will give unto this last, even as unto thee.

15. Is it not lawful for me to do what I will with mine own? Is thine eye evil, because I am good?

16. So the last shall be first, and the first last: for many be called, but few chosen.

This is the last of the parables that teaches accountability and reward. It introduces two additional elements to the concepts covered in the talents and pounds. First, the spirit in which you perform your labors in the kingdom of God will be taken into consideration on judgment day. Second, the reward will be universal, regardless of the length of time spent laboring.

The setting of the parable is important to its interpretation. The Lord had been giving instructions to his disciples and had been asked by a rich young ruler how he could attain eternal life. The ensuing discussion led to the conclusion that the ruler must sell all that he had, give it to the poor, and follow Jesus. The rich man could not comply with this request and sadly went his way, for "he had great possessions" (Matthew 19:22). Jesus then declared that it would be very difficult for people who were wealthy in things pertaining to the world to enter into the kingdom of God. The disciples were exceedingly amazed at his statement and asked, "Who then can be saved?" (Matthew 19:25.) To the question, Jesus calmly responded that all things were possible. Then Peter, speaking for himself and presumably for all of the Twelve asked, "Behold, we have forsaken all, and followed thee; what shall we have therefore?" (Matthew 19:27.)

Jesus acknowledged their devotion and assured them that their sacrifices and continued labor would entitle them to sit upon thrones in the kingdom of his Father. But he cautioned them that "many that are first shall be last; and the last shall be first" (Matthew 19:30). He then gave the parable of the labourers in the vineyard.

This parable was a direct answer to Peter's question and an example of the philosophy of the Jewish rulers of the time. They believed that they earned rewards in the kingdom of heaven through their labors on the earth, and that the greater the labor, the greater the reward. This belief overlooked some of the factors in the equation, including that of the grace of God. The Lord did not want this concept to carry over into the teachings of the gospel, and through this parable he essentially declared that "he who works in my kingdom for the sake of a reward hereafter, may do his work well, but he honours me less than others who trust in me without thinking of future gain."[25]

This parable was a warning that the spirit in which one labors for the kingdom is what gives the service its value, and the answer to Peter's question indicated that just because the Twelve had been called first to the work, they should not necessarily trust in that call to insure their reward.[26] They were not to be boastful or proud in the work they performed, nor to compete in order to assert themselves one above another.[27]

This parable, like that of the talents, is also set forth in scenes. In the first scene a householder goes out early in the day to hire men to work in his vineyard. The householder is representative of God, and the labourers might well have represented Peter and the others who had just asked the question, "What shall we have therefore?" The Lord in the parable "agreed with the labourers for a penny a day," thus establishing their wages at the outset of their work.

As the day progressed the householder continued his solicitation for laborers, and at the third hour he hired others and told them to go into the vineyard to labor. However, this time, instead of bargaining with them for their reward, the Lord merely stated, "Whatsoever is right I will give you," and the laborers were satisfied to trust in the goodness of the householder.

Again the householder went out in the sixth and the ninth hours and hired additional laborers. To emphasize the teaching of the parable Jesus had the householder go out even in the eleventh hour, and still finding potential laborers, he asked why they were standing idle. They were idle not because they did not want to work, but because no one had hired them. The householder immediately told them to go into the vineyard and work, saying, "Whatsoever is right, that shall ye receive." The hiring of different laborers at different hours indicated the abundance of work that was available in the vineyard and the anxiety of the householder to get all of the available laborers in order that the work could be accomplished.[28]

The laborers could have refused the opportunity to labor, but did not. Those called first bargained for their wages, and an amount was promised and agreed upon. Those later called into the ministry did not bargain for their labors but relied upon the goodness and mercy of the householder, knowing that he was just and that they would be paid fairly.

In the second (and last) scene of the parable, the householder called for the laborers to come forth and give an account of their labor, that they might receive the reward for their hire. But instead of calling those who had been hired first, the householder called those who were hired in the eleventh hour so that they might be paid first. (This was again a direct application to Peter's question and the Lord's answer.)

The laborers called first to receive payment had to rely on the mercy of the master for their wages, as did all the other men who had been hired after the first hour. Those who had been hired early and had negotiated their wages watched as the householder paid all the other laborers a penny for their work, regardless of the length of time they had labored. In view of this they felt they were entitled to more than a penny for their long hours, and keenly anticipated a greater reward from the householder. But when the master got to them he paid them only the penny that had been agreed upon, and they murmured against the master because they felt that since they had "borne the burden and heat of the day," they were entitled to additional wages.

Their petition intimated that an injustice had been done, for they felt that the labor performed did not compare with the wages received. But this was exactly the point of the parable. The laborers of the morning claimed injustice, but had received just the opposite. They were paid exactly what they had bargained for. The others received the same pay, because it was all that the Lord had to give. Each servant in turn, whether among those who were first called to the service or those who were called last, had the same opportunity to gain the reward. That reward (the only reward that is available) is entrance into the kingdom of God and the receipt of all that the Father has, even joint heirship with Jesus Christ (Romans 8:16–17).[29] Once a servant accepted the call, the work he performed up to the time of accountability would be sufficient for him to enter into the kingdom of God—providing he performed it with all faithful diligence and devotion to God.

The Lord reminded those who objected to their reward that it was lawful for him to do with his own that which he would, and he asked them if they were behaving evilly because he had been good. He again reiterated that the last shall be first and the first last, for many were called, but few chosen. This warning indicated that "those who seem chiefest in [the] labor, yet . . . may altogether lose the things which they have wrought; and those who seem last, may, by keeping their humility, be acknowledged first in the day of God."[30] The kingdom of heaven is God's to give. The reckoning of man's stewardship will be determined by *how* he performs his labors as much as *whether* he performs his labors.

In the parables of the talents and the pounds, the ultimate question of accountability was whether any labor had been performed at all. Now, in addition to that consideration, accountability included whether the labors had been performed with the proper spirit. If not, perhaps there was a risk that the reward could be lost, for "the kingdom of heaven is not a matter of mercenary calculation or exact equivalent—there [is] no bargaining with the Heavenly Householder."[31] In the parable the reward was a gift from God, and *not a payment of debt* as a result of the labors of the servants.[32]

It is not when we are called to serve the Lord that determines our reward, but how we serve him. Those called late in life to the service who serve well will stand equal with and perhaps above those who are called early, but serve poorly. A story elucidating this principle deals with Thomas after the resurrection of Jesus. Jesus had appeared to the Apostles when Thomas was not with them. They later told Thomas that the Lord had risen. Instead of readily accepting the testimony of his fellow Apostles, Thomas said that he could not believe until he had seen the Lord personally, and placed his fingers in the prints of the nails and thrust his hand into his side. Eight days later the Lord again appeared to the Apostles; this time Thomas was with them. Jesus instructed Thomas to "reach hither thy finger, and behold my hands; and reach hither thy hand, and thrust it into my side: and be not faithless, but believing" (John 20:27). Thomas did so and acknowledged the Savior. Jesus then said, "Because thou hast seen me, thou hast believed: blessed are they that have not seen, and yet have believed" (John 20:29).

The vineyard in the parable was the kingdom of God on earth. The laborers represented the servants of the Lord, and

Jesus was the husbandman. The parable can apply to those who are outside the Church and converted late in life, as well as to those who are already members of the Church but have not done the Lord's bidding, and who, after repentance, accept the call and find their work graciously accepted.

The laborers that were hired early to work in the master's vineyard bargained for their reward and afterward received what they had bargained for, but with grumbling and murmuring. Other laborers, hired later, relied on the grace and mercy of the Lord to give that which was just for their labors. The complaining and the bickering of the first laborers bespoke their mental and moral unfitness.[33]

Modern scripture explains the reasons for the grumbling and complaints and potential loss of reward, even though the servants labored all day long. The Lord noted that many were called and few were chosen. Modern revelation continues: "And why are they not chosen? Because their hearts are set so much upon the things of this world, and aspire to the honors of men." (D&C 121:34–35.) Hence the moral of the reward is taught. There is no precise equation between the work done and the reward received. We receive the reward through the grace of God because he has promised it, not just because we have earned it (Ephesians 2:4–10; Moroni 10:32–33).[34]

Part Five

Teaching Warnings and Judgment

Parables That Teach Warnings 9

The Lord wants everyone to live the gospel requirements and acquire his promised blessings. But he warned of potential failure. The Jews belonged to a favored race, the people of Israel. This esteemed position led them to believe that they were automatically entitled to the promised kingdom. But it was not to be so.

The things of the world can blind a person to spiritual decisions. And even when living within the parameters of the gospel's teachings, all of the Lord's children must be cautious so that their humility and meekness are not overcome.

The Foolish Rich Man

Luke 12:13–21

13. And one of the company said unto him, Master, speak to my brother, that he divide the inheritance with me.

14. And he said unto him, Man, who made me a judge or a divider over you?

15. And he said unto them, Take heed, and beware of covetousness: for a man's life consisteth not in

the abundance of the things
which he possesseth.
16. And he spake a parable unto them, saying, The
ground of a certain rich man
brought forth plentifully:
17. And he thought
within himself, saying, What
shall I do, because I have no
room where to bestow my
fruits?
18. And he said, This
will I do: I will pull down
my barns, and build greater;
and there will I bestow all
my fruits and my goods.
19. And I will say to my
soul, Soul, thou hast much
goods laid up for many
years; take thine ease, eat,
drink, and be merry.
20. But God said unto
him, Thou fool, this night
thy soul shall be required of
thee: then whose shall those
things be, which thou hast
provided?
21. So is he that layeth
up treasure for himself, and
is not rich toward God.

The twelfth chapter of Luke is a teaching unit based on the theme of godliness as contrasted with worldliness. (These same concepts appear in widely divergent sections of the other Gospels.)[1] Like many other parts of Luke's Gospel, this parable is set in a real-life situation that gives added insight into the Lord's character and reputation. Luke did not identify the whereabouts of Jesus on this occasion, but the Lord was teaching his Apostles and others when he was interrupted by a man in the crowd. The intruder was apparently totally disinterested in the spiritual truths that the Lord was teaching, and interrupted him with a selfish, secular question.

The man asked the Lord to intervene in an inheritance problem between himself and his brother. The Jewish law on inheritance was clearly defined, and it can be assumed that the man had no just legal claim or he would not have appealed to Jesus.[2] But the fact that he did gives insight into the stature the Lord had attained by this time in his ministry.

The Savior treated the man's question with complete forthrightness, stating that he would not act as judge between the man and his brother. He warned the man and those who had drawn close around him about their covetous nature, having their hearts set only upon the things of the world. After this admonition Jesus taught the parable of the foolish rich man to warn the individual about the relationship between worldly things and the things of the spirit.

The Lord began the parable by declaring that during the harvest the ground of a certain man brought forth an unanticipated abundance of good. The man wondered what he should do with his newfound wealth. He had always been obsessed with the accumulation of worldly things, and was concerned about how he should preserve his huge surplus. This reaction is characteristic of a covetous man.[3] His thoughts and actions were centered around how he could secure his personal ease and sensuous enjoyment.[4] His heart was proud, selfish, and self-indulgent, and he considered his carefully planned future as if it were a foregone conclusion.

The Lord purposely embodied in this wealthy man the selfish propensities he was warning against. The man, by his declarations, admitted that the innermost thoughts of his heart were set upon his provisions for the flesh.[5] His plans stretched no higher than to satisfy his earthly desires, and he failed in all particulars to include God in his gain.[6] He had placed the things of the world above the worship of God, and thus had broken the first great commandment. In addition, he had decided to use his abundance for his personal, selfish, and lustful desires rather than in the service of his fellowman—thus breaking the second great commandment. Although he was laying up in abundance worldly things, he was impoverished spiritually (Matthew 6:20–21).[7] Then the Lord gave the warning of the parable when he said to the man, "Thou fool, this night thy soul shall be required of thee."

This is an interesting use of the word *fool.* The Psalmist had recorded many centuries before, "The fool hath said in his heart, There is no God" (Psalm 14:1), thus emphasizing the biblical meaning of the word *fool* as "a man who practically denies the existence of God."[8]

The emphasis of the parable thus far had been on the relationship between the laying up of spiritual versus worldly treasures, and the competition between them. Now it shifted to a warning about making the wrong choice. It was not the imminent death of the individual, but his impending judgment that the Lord warned of. The man had carefully assessed his personal situation and judged his needs, but had made the wrong choice. "Whose shall those things be, which thou hast provided?" the Lord then asked in the parable. All that the man had accounted so dear, all that he determined he would profit by, was now for naught. The author of Ecclesiastes had warned, "He that loveth silver shall not be satisfied with silver; nor he that loveth abundance with increase: this is also vanity" (Ecclesiastes 5:10). The rich man had emphasized all the wrong things (self, world, riches), and had forgotten all the right ones (God, his neighbor, the poor).

The relationship was perfectly clear: "The man whose treasure is of earth leaves it all at death; he whose wealth is in heaven goes to his own, and death is but the portal to his treasury."[9] The Talmud records "that a Rabbi told his disciples, 'Repent the day before thy death;' and when his disciples asked him: 'Does a man know the day of his death?' he replied, that on that very ground he should repent to-day, lest he should die to-morrow. And so would all his days be days of repentance."[10]

Our personal pathway to the kingdom of God is one of choices, and the parable emphatically warned that we would be judged according to those selections. "How brief, yet how rich in significance, is that little parable which He told them, of the rich fool who, in his greedy, God-forgetting, presumptuous selfishness, would do this and that . . . who . . . thought that 'my fruits,' and 'my goods,' and 'my barns,' and to 'eat and drink and be merry' could for many years . . . sustain what was left him of a soul, but to whom from heaven pealed as a terrible echo to his words, the heart-thrilling sentence of awful irony, *'Thou fool, this night!'* "[11]

After giving the parable, Jesus finished his instructions by concluding, "For all these things do the nations of the world seek after: and your Father knoweth that ye have need of these things. But rather seek ye the kingdom of God; and all these things shall be added unto you." (Luke 12:30–31.)

Paul, to the Romans, expanded the warning when he declared, "But put ye on the Lord Jesus Christ, and make not provision for the flesh, to fulfill the lusts thereof" (Romans 13:14)—a strong warning for each of God's children.

The Pharisee and the Publican

Luke 18:9–14

9. And he spake this parable unto certain which trusted in themselves that they were righteous, and despised others:
10. Two men went up into the temple to pray; the one a Pharisee, and the other a publican.
11. The Pharisee stood and prayed thus with himself, God, I thank thee, that I am not as other men are, extortioners, unjust, adulterers, or even as this publican.
12. I fast twice in the week, I give tithes of all that I possess.
13. And the publican, standing afar off, would not lift up so much as his eyes unto heaven, but smote upon his breast, saying, God be merciful to me a sinner.
14. I tell you, this man went down to his house justified rather than the other: for every one that exalteth himself shall be abased; and he that humbleth himself shall be exalted.

This is another of those little parables given as a direct caution and warning. In the parable of the rich fool the Lord had declared his warning with regard to the individual's choices between worldliness and spirituality. Now the Lord would, in parabolic form, warn those of the covenant who "trusted in themselves that they were righteous, and despised others."

The characters in the parable are a Pharisee and a publican. Although the Lord selected these character-types for use in the parable, the parable was not addressed to Pharisees and publicans exclusively.[12] The parable was a general warning to all those within the covenant, and is as applicable today as it was at the time Jesus gave it. The message of the parable is depicted through the prayers of the Pharisee and the publican, but it is not the principle of prayer that is being taught. The prayers are simply the tools used by the Lord to teach the principle and warn against self-righteousness within the kingdom.[13]

The Pharisee stood as he prayed. This was one position for prayer used by the Jews and Israelites of old. (1 Kings 8:22;

Matthew 6:5). Sometimes, perhaps in moments of greater humility and supplication, they knelt (Daniel 6:10; 2 Chronicles 6:13; Psalm 95:6). The early moments of the Pharisee's prayer showed promise, but his thanksgiving quickly deteriorated. He offered only a proud, cold thanks for his own merits while emulating the lifeless formality of the rabbis of his day. "The religion of the day was so largely mechanical, that they were in danger of mistaking the outward form for the substance."[14]

In his "righteous observance" of the Law, the Pharisee sought only self-justification in his excessive zeal and assurance that he would be separated from sinners. He thanked God that he was not as those whom he looked down upon, and he felt nothing but contempt for those in a class lower than his. Perhaps as he prayed he cast his eyes upon the publican and now, along with all others he despised, he dragged him into his prayer as one whom he held in contempt.

He declared his righteousness openly. He fasted twice a week, whereas Rabbinical Law demanded only once a year (based on Leviticus 16:29).[15] He tithed all he possessed, rather than that which he earned annually, as the Law required.[16] (Deuteronomy 14:22; Leviticus 27:30.) He would have God as his debtor, and confessed none of his sins or inadequacies before him.

The Lord now placed the publican in direct contrast with the Pharisee. The publican stood afar off, not wanting to press near the holy place, even though as a Jew he had the right to be there. In reverence he smote upon his chest, a sign of his inward grief, and begged the mercy of God. He was overwhelmed by the bitter sense of his distance from God. Under the Jewish Law his calling placed him and his family in a hopeless position, yet his prayer indicated that he was in the process of repentance.[17]

After drawing this parabolic picture, the Lord quickly concluded by issuing a warning that may have completely overwhelmed his audience. The parable disclosed that the publican, rather than the Pharisee, departed to his house justified. Those who exalted themselves under the Law would be abased, and those who humbled themselves would be exalted.[18] The Pharisee departed justified only before men, prouder than ever of his haughty observance of a dead and cold Law. The publican went away hated by man, but justified before God.[19]

The covenant people who used the Law merely to fulfill social needs, to gain personal gratification, or to be visibly self-righteous had been warned. God would reject the self-righteous, but his mercy would be boundless to those who came to him with a broken heart and a contrite spirit.

The Barren Fig Tree

Luke 13:6–9

6. He spake also this parable; A certain man had a fig tree planted in his vineyard; and he came and sought fruit thereon, and found none.

7. Then said he unto the dresser of his vineyard, Behold, these three years I come seeking fruit on this fig tree, and find none: cut it down; why cumbereth it the ground?

8. And he answering said unto him, Lord, let it alone this year also, till I shall dig about it, and dung it:

9. And if it bear fruit, well: and if not, then after that thou shalt cut it down.

This was the last of the warning parables and it was directed to Israel as a nation. The essence of this parable was that the salt had lost its savor and was thenceforth good for nothing and should be cast out and trodden under foot of man (Matthew 5:13).[20]

Before teaching this parable, Jesus had been told of a terrible calamity that had befallen certain Galileans. Their blood had been mingled with pagan sacrifices by Pilate, and Jesus, in response to this story, asked if the people thought that this made those Galileans sinners above all Galileans (Luke 13:1–2). Then he raised the example of the eighteen upon whom the tower in Siloam had fallen (Luke 13:4–5). He noted that these were merely calamities of life, and that although sin and suffering might be generally related, it was not always possible to link individual sin to a given disaster. Rather, disasters were usually the result of life's circumstances.

The focus in this parable should not be on the sins of others but on our own sins, and the eternal calamity which will befall us if we do not repent. It concerns both the long-suffering and the severity of God.

As the parable began, a certain man (representing God) owned a fig tree. When he came to see how much fruit the tree had produced, none was found. Apparently this had occurred for a period of three years and the owner of the vineyard instructed his dresser to cut the tree down, that it might no longer encumber the ground. This was all done in accordance with the traditional law of the people, for "a barren tree would be of threefold disadvantage: it would yield no fruit; it would fill valuable space, which a fruit-bearer might occupy; and it would needlessly deteriorate the land. Accordingly, while it was forbidden to destroy fruit-bearing trees, it would, on the grounds above stated, be duty to cut down a 'barren' . . . tree."[21]

In the parable the fig tree, long an emblem of the Jewish nation (Joel 1:7; Jacob 5), represented Israel. Man's actions and attitudes (his works) toward the kingdom of God were often compared to the production of fruit (Psalm 1:3; John 15:2–5; Romans 7:4). Three kinds of actions, or works, were commonly referred to: First were good works, for the tree bearing good fruit represented those who were categorized as bringing forth good works. Second were dead works, wherein people acted in conformity with the Law but in form only, and not for the glory of God. Third were evil works, wherein a corrupt tree brought forth corrupt fruit.[22]

Upon being ordered to cut the tree down, the dresser of the vineyard (representing the Savior) requested that one more year be given to determine whether the tree would bring forth fruit. He said he would "dig about it, and dung it" during that period of time, to see if the tree would produce. Such a request for the deferment of God's judgment was not uncommon (2 Peter 3:9). Thus, additional time would be given and the punishment prescribed in the parable would be deferred in order to grant an additional period of time for repentance.[23]

The pleading by the dresser of the vineyard depicts Jesus in his role as our intercessor with the Father. But he agreed that if the tree did not bear fruit this time, it would be cut down and destroyed.

The symbolism of the parable could not have been missed by those who heard it. The announcement of a judgment and then the suspension of the sentence to allow one more attempt at repentance was a process familiar to the leadership of the Jews. Noah had preached and prophesied before the Flood, and other eminent prophets appeared prior to the great catastrophes suffered by Israel. God's impatience had been graphically depicted before their eyes.

Although the Israelites had been chosen as God's elect, that election did not guarantee them the kingdom; it was merely a means to that end. If the tree bore not good fruit, it would be cut out and discarded. The time had come for Israel to determine whether it would accept God or its inevitable destruction. Although time would be granted for repentance, the destruction of the tree that would not bring forth good fruit was decreed. The warning to the chosen people had been given.[24]

Parables That Teach Judgment 10

Christ's gospel established the requirements for entry into the kingdom of God. It provided laws and ordinances whereby all mankind would be judged and could be saved. That the judgment would be fair was beyond doubt, for all judgment was entrusted to Jesus Christ. The standards were well-defined, and the entire population of the world would ultimately be judged by them. This chapter deals with the parables that taught of this judgment.

To the Rulers of Israel

The Wicked Husbandman

Matthew 21:33–41

33. Hear another parable: There was a certain householder, which planted a vineyard, and hedged it round about, and digged a winepress in it, and built a tower, and let it out to husbandmen, and went into a far country:

34. And when the time of the fruit drew near, he sent his servants to the hus-

bandmen, that they might receive the fruits of it.

35. And the husbandmen took his servants, and beat one, and killed another, and stoned another.

36. Again, he sent other servants more than the first: and they did unto them likewise.

37. But last of all he sent unto them his son, saying, They will reverence my son.

38. But when the husbandmen saw the son, they said among themselves, This is the heir; come, let us kill him, and let us seize on his inheritance.

39. And they caught him, and cast him out of the vineyard, and slew him.

40. When the lord therefore of the vineyard cometh, what will he do unto those husbandmen?

41. They say unto him, He will miserably destroy those wicked men, and will let out his vineyard unto other husbandmen, which shall render him the fruits in their seasons.

Cross-references

Mark 12:1–9 Luke 20:9–16

This is one of the few parables recorded in all three Synoptics. The three versions differ slightly, due to their independent authors, but they do not disagree in any of the significant points of the parable. All three writers agree that Jesus was teaching the people in the presence of the Pharisees and the rulers of the Jews. These men had come to Jesus and asked him by what authority he taught the people. He, in turn, asked them concerning the authority of John, and they refused to answer whether it was from God or from man, but rather indicated that they could not tell. Jesus likewise refused to declare his authority, but taught them this parable instead.[1]

The parable is historical in nature, in one sense describing God's relationship to the chosen people from Israel to Christ, and in a larger sense describing his relationship with the entire human family from Adam to the Second Coming.[2] It is judgmental in its conclusion, and could be considered to be both descriptive of an existing situation and prophetic of a future one.[3] The story is told in a realistic manner and would have been recognized and understood by the rulers of the Jews, as all three Synoptics attest.

The opening words of the parable are similar to those of Isaiah in his song of the vineyard (Isaiah 5), wherein the house of Israel is portrayed as the vine stock, or a vineyard (a common analogy in the Old Testament—see Psalm 80:8–16; Isaiah 5:1–7; 27:1–7; Jeremiah 2:21).

The symbolism of the parable and its principal parts are as follows:

The householder—the owner of the vineyard, representing God.

The vineyard—could be considered generally as the human family, but specifically as the house of Israel.

The embellishment of the vineyard (hedged about, digged around, tower provided)—the covenant established between God and Israel that made Israel distinct and separate from other nations and chosen above all other people.[4]

The husbandmen—might have symbolically referred to the nation of Israel and its responsibility to the rest of mankind, but specifically referred to the spiritual overseers or ecclesiastical leaders of Israel.[5]

The far country—God departing and leaving the vineyard (or the children of men) in the hands of the religious leaders.

The servants—the prophets who came to the children of Israel in the name of God.

The son—Jesus Christ.

The fruits—the souls of men brought into the kingdom of God through instruction, repentance, and adherence to the commandments.[6]

Although the vineyard in this parable was planted by the householder, it was let out to certain husbandmen (representing the leadership of Israel). They were given charge of the vineyard as part of their commission (Ezekiel 34:1–11; Malachi 2:1–10). The lord of the vineyard, or the householder, then withdrew and awaited the growth of the fruit. When the harvest season arrived, the householder sent a servant that he might collect and receive of the fruit of the vineyard. This represented the prophets who were sent by God to call the children of Israel to repentance, teach them the errors of their ways, and encourage them to return to his kingdom. Luke indicates that the servants were sent three times, while Mark and Matthew add that many others were also sent. But rather than being glad, the leaders of Israel received the prophets with disdain and hatred. They beat, wounded, and shamefully mistreated them, stoning some and killing others.[7]

The patience of the householder is clearly depicted in this parabolic story. Even though the servants (or prophets) were evilly mistreated, the householder, in his goodness, continued to send others. He did this for two reasons: first, so that adequate time might be allowed to recover God's children; and second, to show that the rebellious children and wicked overseers had time after time rejected the call to repentance, and by so doing would suffer the consequences of their actions.

After the rejection and abuse of the prophets had taken place, the householder sent his son, the long-awaited Messiah. For surely, he said, "they will reverence my son." But instead of reverencing the son, they came out in open rebellion against him. The last effort of God's divine mercy was rejected, and the vineyard ripened in sin. The husbandmen said to themselves, "This is the heir; come, let us kill him, and let us seize on his inheritance."

The husbandmen of the vineyard thought they could defeat the purpose of God by killing his son; but rather than defeat God's purpose, they would help to bring it about. This portion of the parable is prophetic, for the death of the Savior had not yet occurred. However, the die had been cast, so that he could predict that they would indeed cast out the son and kill him.

After Jesus finished telling the parable he applied it directly to the rulers of the Jews and let them publicly judge themselves. He asked them a question: "When the lord therefore of the vineyard cometh, what will he do unto those husbandmen?" The Jewish rulers generally attempted to avoid questions put to them by the Lord, and had just recently avoided the question of John's authority, but they could not avoid this question. They were standing before the people, so they answered the only way they could. "They say unto him, He will miserably destroy those wicked men, and will let out his vineyard unto other husbandmen, which shall render him the fruits in their seasons."

Luke's account tells us that, immediately recognizing the application of the parable, they exclaimed, "God forbid." They knew that the Lord was applying the parable to them, that he was predicting their rejection and ultimate destruction and the end of Israel's favored position—that the kingdom was to be given to another nation, one that would bring forth the fruits demanded by the householder. Their wickedness and disobedience had been graphically portrayed in the parable. "They had been entrusted with a valuable institution; an elect nation furnished with good laws . . . speaking generally, they had lost sight of the end of Israel's calling. . . . They had occupied their position for their own glory . . . they had neglected the vineyard . . . thinking only of privilege and forgetting duty."[8]

To emphasize to his listeners that he was the "son" of the parable, whom they had rejected, the Lord answered their exclamation with a recognizable Messianic scripture. "The stone which the builders rejected, the same is become the head of the corner" (Matthew 21:42). It was an Old Testament quotation specifically referring to the Messianic claim (Psalm 118:22). By its use Jesus openly called himself the Son of God, the expected Messiah.

He now warned the rulers of the Jews of their impending judgment. He stated that whosoever fell upon the stone would be broken, and on whomsoever it should fall, it would grind them to powder. He went beyond the analogy of the parable and made an open declaration of his Messiahship, at the same time emphasizing the malice of the Pharisees. He told them that they could not defeat the purposes of God. He warned them that they had already stumbled at the stone and were about to be crushed by it because they had deliberately set themselves in opposition to him, knowing who he was (Matthew 21:44).

There is no question that the Pharisees and the rulers of the Jews knew and understood the application of this parable. All three of the Synoptics declare that they knew that he spoke of them. Their reaction clearly indicates this, for they sought how they might lay hands on him; they sent spies that they might take hold of his words, and they sent other Pharisees and Herodians to catch him in his words (Mark 12:13).

Their rage at Christ's candor concerning their wickedness was thwarted, for the scriptures note that they would not lay hands on him because they feared the people, who thought Jesus was a prophet (Matthew 21:46). Although they had understood and perceived the meaning of other parables, they "saw now, more clearly than ever, the whole bent and drift of these parables, and longed for the hour of vengeance! . . . He had depicted the trust and responsibility of their office, and had indicated a terrible retribution for its cruel and profligate abuse."[9]

They could not claim ignorance, for they had acknowledged their understanding. They could not claim mercy, for they had rejected repentance. They could not claim obedience, for they had stoned and killed the prophets. Their evils and disobedience had culminated in their open rebellion against God, and for it their house would be left desolate.

To the Covenant People

Two parables given by Jesus taught the covenant people of the impending judgment: the parable of the great supper, and the parable of the marriage of the king's son. They deal with the same principle, but produce differing results.

The Great Supper

Luke 14:16—24

16. Then said he unto him, A certain man made a great supper, and bade many:

17. And sent his servant at supper time to say to them that were bidden, Come; for all things are now ready.

18. And they all with one consent began to make excuse. The first said unto him, I have bought a piece of ground, and I must needs go and see it: I pray thee have me excused.

19. And another said, I have bought five yoke of oxen, and I go to prove them: I pray thee have me excused.

20. And another said, I have married a wife, and therefore I cannot come.

21. So that servant came, and shewed his lord these things. Then the master of the house being angry said to his servant, Go out quickly into the streets and lanes of the city, and bring in hither the poor, and the maimed, and the halt, and the blind.

22. And the servant said, Lord, it is done as thou hast

commanded, and yet there is room.

23. And the lord said unto the servant, Go out into the highways and hedges, and compel them to come in, that my house may be filled.

24. For I say unto you, That none of those men which were bidden shall taste of my supper.

The setting of this parable is quite important to its interpretation. During the Perean ministry, Jesus had been invited to the house of one of the chief Pharisees to eat on the Sabbath day. The scripture declares that the Jews invited him that they might watch him (Luke 14:1). (The healing of the man with the dropsy was performed on this occasion.)[10] As the discussion progressed, Jesus gave the parable of the wedding guests as a reprimand to the Jews for their custom of seating people at their feasts according to social stature.[11] He upbraided them for their self-aggrandizement, and the exclusion of the poor and the afflicted. He taught them not to invite the self-indulging rich (in an attempt to climb the social ladder), but to invite the meek and lowly (those of no influence or importance). By so doing, they would receive their compensation at the resurrection of the just (Luke 14:13–14).

Apparently those who heard the Lord did not fully comprehend the parable of the wedding guests, or else they chose to ignore the chastisement it contained, for one of them still gloried in his anticipation of the Messiah's kingdom where the righteous would be invited to sit down at a great supper with Him.[12] The man cried aloud, "Blessed is he that shall eat bread in the kingdom of God" (Luke 14:15). This great feast, "by which the Messianic reign was to be ushered in was a favorite theme of jubilant exposition in both synagog and school; and exultation ran high in the rabbinical dictum that none but the children of Abraham would be among the blessed partakers."[13]

But Jesus would not allow this misunderstanding of both his miracle and his parable; he gave the Pharisees and other guests at the dinner the parable of the great supper as his final teaching of the day.

The parable of the great supper told of a certain man who invited a large number of select guests to come and partake of his sumptuous meal. The customs and traditions of the time were reflected in the story. The guests were invited and given sufficient time to respond to the invitation so that the host could adequately prepare for those who would be in attendance.[14] At the proper time, a servant was sent to tell those who had been bidden that "all things are now ready." Those who had been invited and had accepted could now properly come to the supper, but they began to give excuses, each in his turn, that they might not attend.

The invited guests represented the covenant people of Israel, and the servant sent to bid them to the meal was the Lord, their long-awaited Messiah.[15] The excuses the guests gave represented the Lord's rejection by the covenant people.

The first guest declared that he had purchased a piece of ground and must go and see it—a weak excuse at best, for he had no real desire to go to the feast and no reverence for the host. The possessions of the world had taken precedence over his desire to enter the kingdom.

The second guest had purchased five yoke of oxen and had need to prove them. Again, an excuse of meager importance. This man placed his business endeavors above his respect for his host.

The last guest had married a wife and could not come. Thus the pleasures of social life were represented, for during his marriage celebration he would declare his own feast,[16] placing his own pleasures above his commitment to his host.

The Lord was presenting a concise analogy. Advancement to the kingdom, even for those previously called and separated out from among the people of the world in general, required giving up that which seemed to them necessary and most desirable for their immediate, personal enjoyment.[17]

The guest's activities mentioned as excuses were not in and of themselves sinful, but became so because the guests placed them above their responsibility to the kingdom of God. Paul, perhaps with this parable in mind, cautioned the people about choosing between the things of the world and the kingdom of God when he said, "This I say, brethren, the time is short: it remaineth, that both they that have wives be as though they had none; and they that weep, as though they wept not; and they that rejoice, as though they rejoiced not; and they that buy, as though they possessed not; and they that use this world, as not abusing it: for the fashion of this world passeth away" (1 Corinthians 7:29–31).

After the servant heard all of the guests' excuses, he returned to his lord and told him what they had said. The master became angry and instructed the servant to go quickly into the "streets and lanes of the city, and bring in hither the poor, and the maimed, and the halt, and the blind." The servant complied with his master's instructions, but there was yet room at the supper, and the lord instructed the servant to go out a second time into "the highways and hedges, and compel them to come in," in order that his house would be full. Note that even though these people were invited, they had to be "compelled" to come to the supper. These, it would seem, are those who truly feel unworthy to be in the presence of the Lord. Therefore, they must be persuaded to come and recognize that the benevolence and patience of the householder was intended for them also. This was the most deadly thrust of the parable, for it struck at the most cherished of Jewish prejudices.

The first invitation was given to the poor, the outcast, the sinners and publicans, and the hated multitudes who neglected the rabbinical rules, but were still the covenant people. They gladly accepted the Lord's summons. But more than that, the second invitation to those in the highways and hedges indicated that the covenant, so cherished by the Jews, would now be taken from them and given to the Gentiles and the heathens.[18] The spiritually sick and needy, those abhorred by Israel throughout their history, would now receive the kingdom of God.

This was an irrefutable warning of judgment. The covenant that had bound Israel together as they looked for the anticipated Messiah would now be taken from them and given to another.

> It was the proclamation, once more, of the mighty truth which might well be too hard for those who first heard it, to understand, since it is imperfectly realized after nineteen centuries; that external rites and formal acts are of no value with God, in themselves; that He looks at the conscience alone; that neither circumcision nor sacrifices, nor legal purifications, nor rigid observance of Sabbath laws, nor fasts, but

the state of the heart, determines the relation of man to God.[19]

The one who had sat at meat with Jesus and with exultation proclaimed the anticipated hope to eventually eat bread with the Messiah in the kingdom of God was wrong. Jesus said that to be invited into the kingdom was one thing and to accept the invitation was another, but even that was not enough. The chosen people had to *go to the supper* in order to eat with the king and receive their reward. The parable told them that they had openly rejected the invitation because of their worldly desires: the management of property, the acquisition of riches, and the pursuit of the more sensual comforts of life. All these things were incompatible with the desire to attend the Lord's supper in the kingdom of heaven.

But other invitations were extended. They were given to people who had been excluded by the Jews in their rabbinical sophistry, and to those who had excluded themselves because of their sins. All these were offered the kingdom and, based on their own merits, they would enter before those who "thanked God that they were not as other men."[20]

Now Jesus concluded the parable. To those who refused the Messiah, the host declared that "none of those men which were bidden shall taste of my supper." The contemptuous guests who had initially accepted the Lord's invitation but refused to come when bidden were warned that if they continued to refuse the Messiah, others would take their place and they would not enter into the feast which they had so eagerly anticipated.

The Marriage of the King's Son

Matthew 22:1–14

1. And Jesus answered and spake unto them again by parables, and said,

2. The kingdom of heaven is like unto a certain king, which made a marriage for his son,

3. And sent forth his servants to call them that were bidden to the wedding: and they would not come.

4. Again, he sent forth other servants, saying, Tell them which are bidden,

Behold, I have prepared my dinner: my oxen and my fatlings are killed, and all things are ready: come unto the marriage.

5. But they made light of it, and went their ways, one to his farm, another to his merchandise:

6. And the remnant took his servants, and entreated them spitefully, and slew them.

7. But when the king heard thereof, he was wroth: and he sent forth his armies, and destroyed those murderers, and burned up their city.

8. Then saith he to his servants, The wedding is ready, but they which were bidden were not worthy.

9. Go ye therefore into the highways, and as many as ye shall find, bid to the marriage.

10. So those servants went out into the highways, and gathered together all as many as they found, both bad and good: and the wedding was furnished with guests.

11. And when the king came in to see the guests, he saw there a man which had not on a wedding garment:

12. And he saith unto him, Friend, how camest thou in hither not having a wedding garment? And he was speechless.

13. Then said the king to the servants, Bind him hand and foot, and take him away, and cast him into outer darkness; there shall be weeping and gnashing of teeth.

14. For many are called, but few are chosen.

The Lord gave this parable on the third day of the last week of his life. He was about to close his public ministry and give his last instructions to his Apostles. He would then be betrayed into the hands of his enemies to be crucified before his chosen people. He taught this parable in the temple at a time when the Pharisees and rulers of the Jews had openly declared their hostility and made formal determination to do away with Christ by violent means.

In the parable of the great supper (a parable comparable to this one), a man had arranged for a large meal; now a king would call for the celebration of the marriage of his son. Before, Christ appeared as the servant, being the last of a long line of prophets and teachers. Now he was the founder of a new kingdom, the central person of that kingdom, and the Royal Son (Psalm 72:1). Again the imagery of the parable involved bidding invited guests to come to a feast, just as in the parable of the great supper. Great festivals (Isaiah 25:6; 65:13) and marriage celebrations (Isaiah 61:10; 62:5; Hosea 2:19) were favorite themes of the Jewish rabbis and teachers,[21] and both of these were used in the parable of the marriage of the king's son.

The festive portion of the marriage was traditionally given prominence by the Jews, but here that emphasis is superseded by the conduct of the invited guests. The parable was based on the belief that the Jews would be invited to dine with the Savior in the Messianic kingdom, and that this great festival would usher in the arrival of the Messiah (Zephaniah 1:7). But the kingdom was not to come suddenly, as the Jews expected, for their "invitation" had been issued many centuries before, and now the call to attend the celebration (or enter God's kingdom) was being extended.

That the Jews were God's elect was undisputed, for this position had been emphasized by all the prophets throughout their history. They presumed themselves worthy of entering the Lord's kingdom throughout this entire time; this parable showed that they would make themselves unworthy, for the invited guests (who represented Israel) deliberately rebelled against the authority of the king. The guests proffered feeble reasons to be excused from the banquet, and through their own actions excluded themselves from the very thing they wanted.

At first the guests merely told the servants that they would not come. But in his great patience the Lord again sent forth other servants to tell them that all was ready. He had prepared the dinner and killed the fatlings and bade them come to the marriage. But now the invited guests indicated their total contempt and rejection of the king. They made light of the call and went their ways, considering their personal possessions and affairs more important than the kingdom of God. Some of the guests went one step further and spitefully treated the servants and killed them, coming out in open rebellion and hatred against Him who had made the covenant.

Perhaps the first of these servants to "bid the guests to the wedding" and proclaim the Lord's new kingdom with its anticipated Messiah was John the Baptist. His mission was accomplished during the lifetime of the Lord even though he met a premature end. The Lord received no mistreatment during the commencement of his ministry, but as he proceeded to claim the Messiahship the people openly declared, through their rejection of him, that they would no longer be the people of God. Ultimately their leaders had him crucified.

At this point the king became angry and sent forth his armies to destroy the murderers and burn the guests' city. As in the great supper, the guests who had been originally invited were rejected, but now in a harsher and more permanent manner. The Lord was warning the Jews that unless they repented and accepted him, their swift rejection could carry with it destruction and even death.

Now the king again sent out servants to the highways in order to bring others into the marriage festival. "Both bad and good" were brought in so that the wedding would be furnished with guests (D&C 58:11). Again the doctrine so hateful to the Jews was declared—if they rejected the Lord, the call would go to the Gentiles (Romans 11). And so the hall was filled with guests.

But now the parable indicated that a second judgment would take place. As the guests were brought into the palace they were given special clothing, so that they would be attired in a manner worthy of the king's son (Isaiah 61:10; Zephaniah 1:7–8; Revelation 19:7–9). They could not just sit down at the wedding feast without proper preparation.[22]

Those who had been properly clothed (or properly taught the principles of Christ and his kingdom) had, through repentance, "put on Christ," and adorned themselves as new, spiritual beings through their obedience to his requirements. But one man considered himself worthy to stand before God without the proper preparation, and when he was discovered the king asked him why he was there without the correct attire.[23] Even though the king gave him the opportunity to explain his presence and justify it, the man stood speechless before him. He knew he was not properly prepared to be in the Lord's presence, and he stood condemned.

The unqualified intruder was bound hand and foot, taken

away, and cast out of the kingdom where he, along with those originally invited to the wedding, would not be able to participate in the feast (or the kingdom of God). The Lord concluded the parable by stating, "Many are called, but few are chosen." All mankind are called and eventually given the opportunity to enter the Lord's kingdom, but the chosen are those who, being properly "attired," have met all the requirements of repentance and obedience: Thus, their presence is justified before the Lord.[24]

The warning of judgment about to come upon Israel, which had been alluded to in the parable of the great supper, was now openly declared to the people and the rulers of the Jews in the parable of the marriage of the king's son. The guests had rejected the kingdom and openly showed their hatred toward the king's son (or the Messiah) by killing the servants of the king. Later scriptures support this prophesied rejection (Acts 4:3; 5:18, 40; 7:58; 8:3; 12:3; 14:5; 17:5; 19:24–31; 21:30–32; 23:2).

The parable of the great supper threatened the invited guests with exclusion from the feast, but the marriage of the king's son taught them that they would be destroyed by the king for their rejection of the Son. By their open enmity toward him they condemned themselves. Those who had thought themselves worthy had now proven themselves unworthy. Those who thought only to exalt themselves would now be abased. The covenant they so exclusively cherished would now be offered to all mankind, that through repentance and obedience all could be properly attired and received at the wedding feast to dine with the Son.

The warnings of impending judgment upon the covenant people were complete, and the Jews recognized their application. At the conclusion of this parable the Pharisees "took counsel how they might entangle him [Jesus] in his talk" (Matthew 22:15). They did this that they might justify themselves for putting him to death.

God established his kingdom through his Son, and offered it to the chosen people. He would now "call the heathen to a share in it, while the people of Israel, with their religious leaders . . . had rejected His repeated invitations [and] would no longer be the one people of God."[25]

Conclusion

Because of the similarity between the two parables (the great supper and the marriage of the king's son) there is a temptation to treat them exactly alike. Although they have reference to the same principle, there are significant and substantial differences between them.

It is interesting to make a direct comparison of the parables in order to have their similarities and differences clearly in mind.

The parable of the great supper:	The parable of the king's son:
• Location/time: during the Perean ministry. The Perean ministry extended from the feast of the tabernacles to the week preceding the Lord's last Passover and was cut in half by Christ's visit to Jerusalem during the Feast of Dedication. It was a six-month ministry to Peraea. This parable took place during the last three months, after the Feast of Dedication; thus it was sometime between December and April of the last year of the Lord's ministry.[26]	• Location/time: given by Jesus in the temple on the third day of the last week of his life.
• Giver of the feast: a man (apparently for himself).	• Giver of the feast: a king for the marriage of his son.
• Invited guests: all guests had previously been invited and had formally replied, which was a normal custom of the times.	• Invited guests: all guests had previously been invited and had formally replied.

• Servants sent to declare all things now ready.	• Servants sent to declare that the wedding would commence. Guests would not come.
• Excuses made: a. bought a piece of ground and must see it; b. bought five yoke of oxen and must prove them; c. married a wife and cannot come.	
	• Second group of servants sent: Declared all things for dinner and marriage were ready, bade guests to come.
	• Excuses made: a. made light of invitation and went their way, one to his farm, one to his merchandise; b. remnant refused servants, treated them spitefully, killed them.
• Man was told of refusals, became angry, but made no retribution.	• King became wroth at refusals and violence; sent armies, destroyed those who murdered servants and burned their city.
• Man directed servants to bring in other guests from streets and lanes of the city: the poor, the maimed, the halt, the blind.	• Servants instructed that invited guests were not worthy. Sent for other guests: a. as many as found on highway bade to marriage; b. bad and good invited.
• More room available at feast.	

• Servants instructed to go back to highways and hedges. Compelled more guests to come.

• King inspected guests, discovered man without wedding garment.

• Uninvited intruder was questioned, but was speechless.

• Intruder bound and cast out of the wedding.

• Declaration by man: none of those formally invited would taste of his supper.

• Declaration by king: many called but few chosen.

From the parable of the great supper it was clear that a warning had been given to the covenant people of Israel. If they did not accept the invitation to come into the kingdom of God and accept their Messiah, they would be excluded and others brought in to replace them. In the parable of the king's son the Lord determined that the children of the chosen people had rejected him, and rather than merely issue a warning of impending judgment, he portrayed for them the painful result of that judgment. Their exclusion from the supper and the kingdom of God could be final. Because they had abused and killed the servants of God, they would be utterly destroyed, their covenant would be eliminated, and others would take their places.

To the World

The Gospel Net (The Draw Net)

Matthew 13:47—50

47. Again, the kingdom of heaven is like unto a net,

that was cast into the sea,
and gathered of every kind:
48. Which, when it was
full, they drew to shore, and
sat down, and gathered the
good into vessels, but cast
the bad away.
49. So shall it be at the
end of the world: the angels
shall come forth, and sever
the wicked from among the
just,
50. And shall cast them
into the furnace of fire: there
shall be wailing and
gnashing of teeth.

Because of the fisherman's net used in the comparison, this parable would have great meaning to those who heard it. The draw net was leaded at the bottom so that it would drop to the floor of the sea and scrape along the floor as the net was pulled together. Cork held the top of the net on the water's surface so that all that came within the boundaries of the net might be caught into it.[27]

Just as the net gathered all fish that were within its reach, so too will the gospel gather all men. Not just good men of the earth will come within its grasp and be taught the gospel, but all men of whatever nature will be affected. However, how people react to the demands of the kingdom will cause them, through their actions and attitudes, to pass judgment upon themselves. Therefore, the gathering process is nonselective, with the separation of good and evil following at the end of the harvest.

This parable seems to indicate that inclusion within the net (or within the structure of the Lord's kingdom upon the earth) is not enough to guarantee righteousness. Eventually there will be a separation of good and evil.[28] Just as there was a Judas within the Twelve, so also as the gospel would spread throughout mankind there would be bad disciples as well as good gathered to it.

The final separation which takes place in the parable comes at the end of the world,[29] after all the children of God have been given an opportunity to come within the bounds of the net (or receive the gospel) and be taught that there must be a final payment for all sin. This teaches us that although the wicked seem to thrive here in this life, they will not be able to escape the scrutiny of the final judgment[30] which will come to all mankind.[31] The righteous will be taken home, and the wicked "cast away."

The Watching Servants

Luke 12:36–48

36. And ye yourselves like unto men that wait for their lord, when he will return from the wedding; that when he cometh and knocketh, they may open unto him immediately.

37. Blessed are those servants, whom the lord when he cometh shall find watching: verily I say unto you, that he shall gird himself, and make them to sit down to meat, and will come forth and serve them.

38. And if he shall come in the second watch, or come in the third watch, and find them so, blessed are those servants.

39. And this know, that if the goodman of the house had known what hour the thief would come, he would have watched, and not have suffered his house to be broken through.

40. Be ye therefore ready also: for the Son of man cometh at an hour when ye think not.

41. Then Peter said unto him, Lord, speakest thou this parable unto us, or even to all?

42. And the Lord said, Who then is that faithful and wise steward, whom his lord shall make ruler over his household, to give them their portion of meat in due season?

43. Blessed is that servant, whom his lord when he cometh shall find so doing.

44. Of a truth I say unto you, that he will make him ruler over all that he hath.

45. But and if that servant say in his heart, My lord delayeth his coming; and shall begin to beat the menservants and maidens, and to eat and drink, and to be drunken;

46. The lord of that servant will come in a day when he looketh not for him, and at an hour when he is not aware, and will cut him in sunder, and will appoint him his portion with the unbelievers.

47. And that servant, which knew his lord's will, and prepared not himself, neither did according to his will, shall be beaten with many stripes.

48. But he that knew not, and did commit things worthy of stripes, shall be beaten with few stripes. For

unto whomsoever much is given, of him shall be much required: and to whom men have committed much, of him they will ask the more.

Cross-reference

Matthew 24:43–51

This illustration used by the Lord is not generally regarded as a parable, but Peter interpreted it as one when he questioned the Lord, "Lord, speakest thou this parable unto us, or even to all?" Although not phrased in the true style of a parable, this reference has application to all those who would be encompassed within the gospel, as described in the parable of the gospel net.

The master of the house had left to enjoy a wedding celebration and did not indicate the hour of his return. The servants of the master were left with the admonition that they should remain alert and watch for his imminent return. The journey of the master and his return received no emphasis in the parable. The emphasis falls on the faithful servant, who performs his duty throughout the entire absence of the master and is totally prepared for his return.

Others who are also within the kingdom of the master betray his trust in them through their own self-indulgence. The Lord uses a further analogy in the parable itself when he indicates that if a householder knew when a thief or burglar would come to his home, he would be watchful and not allow his house to be broken into. Through this analogy he again admonishes those listening to wait and watch and be prepared for the Son of Man when he comes, for they know not the hour of his coming.

Those servants who are faithful, who watch and perform their duty well regardless of how long the master is gone, will be rewarded. Those who are unfaithful and are not watching, but think that the master has delayed his coming, who mistreat the other servants, and indulge themselves in things that prevent them from faithfully performing their duty, will be cast out by the master upon his return.

The parable gives a general warning that those who deem themselves safely within the gospel net, those entrusted with the kingdom, are not automatically granted salvation. When the master returns he will know those who have successfully cared for his covenant.

Those who have been faithful will receive a just reward, but those who have been unfaithful in their watch will be separated from the faithful and cast out with the unbelievers.

To the Church

The Ten Virgins

Matthew 25:1–13

1. Then shall the kingdom of heaven be likened unto ten virgins, which took their lamps, and went forth to meet the bridegroom.

2. And five of them were wise, and five were foolish.

3. They that were foolish took their lamps, and took no oil with them:

4. But the wise took oil in their vessels with their lamps.

5. While the bridegroom tarried, they all slumbered and slept.

6. And at midnight there was a cry made, Behold, the bridegroom cometh; go ye out to meet him.

7. Then all those virgins arose, and trimmed their lamps.

8. And the foolish said unto the wise, Give us of your oil; for our lamps are gone out.

9. But the wise answered, saying, Not so; lest there be not enough for us and you: but go ye rather to them that sell, and buy for yourselves.

10. And while they went to buy, the bridegroom came; and they that were ready went in with him to the marriage: and the door was shut.

11. Afterward came also the other virgins, saying, Lord, Lord, open to us.

12. But he answered and said, Verily I say unto you, I know you not.

13. Watch therefore, for ye know neither the day nor the hour wherein the Son of man cometh.

Cross-references

D&C 45:56–59; 63:54

This outstanding parable is a culmination of those parables given by the Lord concerning the judgment that would befall mankind prior to entrance into his heavenly kingdom. In the previous parables, Jesus issued warnings to the leaders of Israel and the covenant people as a whole. In the simple parables of the draw net and the watching servants, he gave a general warning to the world. Now that his kingdom had been established on the earth, Jesus also warned its members, so that they might not fall into the same pit that Israel had before them. Simply belonging to his church does not insure residence in his kingdom.[32]

This parable encompasses all of the doctrine taught in the other parables on judgment. The marriage feast and celebration is again used as the analogy, and the invited guests also play a role. The period of delay between the anticipated coming of the Lord and his actual coming is clearly defined, and emphasis is placed on the need for constant personal preparedness. The parable stresses the fact that although judgment can come at many different times during man's sojourn upon the earth, there will eventually be a final consummation of things and a final judgment; that relying upon membership within the covenant is not sufficient, for unless a person has properly prepared himself, he will still be shut out of the kingdom.

The parable was couched in a setting familiar to the Jews. It dealt with the customs and traditions of the marriage ceremony, for "on the evening of the actual marriage, the bride was led from her paternal home to that of her husband."[33] Everyone around would have been in festive array, and as the procession proceeded, they would have risen to salute and honor both the bride and groom.

The parable discloses that in this anxiously waiting group along the route of the procession there awaited ten virgins bearing lamps. "According to Jewish authorities, it was the custom in the East to carry in a bridal procession about ten such lamps . . . since, according to rubric, ten was the number required to be present at any office or ceremony, such as at the benedictions accompanying the marriage-ceremonies."[34] "Even in this number selected by the Lord, it was not accidental, for one of the rules of the law at that period of time was that wherever ten Jews were living in one place there was to be a Synagogue built for worship."[35]

Thus, ten virgins took their lamps and went forth to meet the bridegroom. The bridegroom represented the Son of God, Jesus the Messiah. The virgins represented the "good" members of the Church, those who had been brought within the covenant, who had a pure profession of faith, were guiltless of apostasy before God, and who believe in their hearts that they had the right to be there anticipating the arrival of the bridegroom.[36]

Of the ten virgins, five were classified as foolish and five as wise. All of the virgins possessed lamps and all of them had oil in their lamps. However, five of the virgins had the thoughtfulness to bring with them extra oil, whereas the other five took no extra oil with them. The lamps they carried indicated that they all belonged to the Church and that they had been sufficiently diligent and obedient to be classified as disciples and members of the earthly kingdom.[37]

The foolish virgins were not hypocritical, just negligent. They were not thoroughly diligent in all of their preparations, and might be compared to the rocky soil found in the parable of the four soils[38] wherein the seed sprang up and had initial growth, but as the sun grew hot it was scorched. These virgins openly manifested external profession of the gospel, but they lacked the deep commitment exemplified by the good soil.[39]

The wise virgins, on the other hand, realized that more was necessary than just external obedience to the commandments and the casual heeding of occasional good impulses. The oil, both that which was contained in the lamps and the extra oil carried by the wise virgins, exemplified and represented the personal spiritual preparedness each of the virgins had acquired as she contemplated entrance into the kingdom of God.[40] The oil had been accumulated drop by drop through righteous living and obedience to the commandments.[41]

There now occurred a fateful pause as the bridegroom tarried during the celebration, and the tired virgins slumbered while they awaited him. They had done all that they deemed necessary to be received by the bridegroom, and they did not know how long it would be before he arrived. Perhaps they had heard of his coming for such a long time that the cry of his coming had become meaningless to them, and so they slept.[42]

The tarrying of the bridegroom, like the leaving of the nobleman,[43] represents the space of time allotted before the final judgment. The end of this earthly probation can occur at any moment during one's life, as was evidenced by the parable of the foolish rich man,[44] but eventually a final reckoning will also take place when every soul must answer for himself.[45] Ultimately all must face a final judgment.

The virgins slept until midnight when they were awakened by the cry, "Behold, the bridegroom cometh." The late hour emphasized the unexpectedness of his coming.[46]

The ten virgins arose, trimmed their lamps, and prepared to meet the bridegroom and be admitted to the wedding feast. The wise had sufficient oil to light their way to the marriage, while the foolish discovered that their lamps had gone out and they could not properly meet the bridegroom. They had not complied with the admonition given by Amulek to the people of the Western Hemisphere when he declared: "This life is the time for men to prepare to meet God; yea, behold the day of this life is the day for men to perform their labors. . . . Therefore, I beseech of you that ye do not procrastinate the day of your repentance until the end; for after this day of life, which is given us to prepare for eternity, behold . . . then cometh the night of darkness wherein there can be no labor performed." (Alma 34:32–33.)

It was not lack of perseverance that had brought the five foolish virgins to this state, but the absence of their personal preparedness. Their overt obedience to the Lord's commandments had been the same as that of the five wise virgins. However, their spiritual commitment, the motivation behind their obedience, was found lacking.

The foolish virgins now did what most of us would do in a like situation. They asked the five prepared virgins to share their oil with them. The wise virgins replied in the only way they could: They said no, "lest there be not enough for us and you," and they told the foolish virgins to go and buy more oil from those who sold it.

No unchristianlike conduct can be imputed to the five wise virgins for refusing to help their foolish sisters, for that was not the intent or the purpose of the parable. Just the opposite was true. Their refusal to share their oil emphasized the proper source of the oil. How can one share his testimony, his willingness to pay tithing, his knowledge, temple work, or any of the other spiritual commitments which must be made in order to properly prepare for the coming of the Savior?[47]

It was already too late for the foolish virgins. They left to find more oil, but while they were gone the bridegroom came, welcomed the prepared virgins into the wedding, and closed the door. Spiritual preparedness cannot be shared at the last minute, nor can a mere request make up for previous unpreparedness. The five foolish virgins returned and knocked on the door, anticipating the mercy of the Lord to allow them entrance. But as with the improperly clothed guest at the marriage of the king's son, the time had passed for preparation and the Lord refused them entry. Those who thought they were close to the kingdom of God missed it after all.

Tennyson exquisitely captured in poetry the thoughts of the virgins who failed in their preparation when he wrote of Guinevere and her contrition. As her remorse swept over her she requested her attentive maiden to sing, and in that moment she painfully recognized her own lack of preparedness as the maiden sang:

> Late, late, so late! and dark the night and chill!
> Late, late, so late! but we can enter still!
> Too late, too late, we cannot enter now.
>
> No light had we; for that we do repent;
> And learning this the bridegroom will relent.
> Too late, too late! ye cannot enter now.
>
> No light; so late! and dark and chill the night!
> O, let us in, that we may find the light!
> Too late, too late: ye cannot enter now.
>
> Have we not heard the bridegroom is so sweet?
> O, let us in tho' late, to kiss his feet!
> No, no, too late! ye cannot enter now.[48]

The reward of the wise virgins was obvious, for they were received into the presence of the bridegroom and the kingdom of heaven. It is said of them, "For they that are wise and have received the truth, and have taken the Holy Spirit for their guide, and have not been deceived . . . shall abide the day" (D&C 45:57).

The Lord concludes the parable with this solemn warning: "Watch therefore, for ye know neither the day nor the hour wherein the Son of man cometh." It was a warning that judgment can come on any day—at any hour—and we are required to be ready, for "that which should have been the work of a life cannot be huddled into a moment."[49]

All of the virgins thought they were properly prepared and would be accepted by the bridegroom. Did not membership in the Church promise such reward? But at that day the delay of his coming may strain even the patience of members of the Church, for none know the hour or the day of his coming. He "cometh as a thief in the night" (1 Thessalonians 5:2), and those who await him may become weary and "sleep."

The five wise virgins slept with that peace of mind acquired through a constant "repentant attitude, seeking forgiveness of sins both large and small, and thus coming ever closer to God. For Church members this is the essence of their preparation, their readiness to meet the Savior when he comes. Any other course will align them with the five foolish virgins in the Master's parable."[50]

Part Six

Witnessing Jesus the Messiah

They Ask of Him a Sign

11

The principles, ordinances, and laws that make up the gospel have been taught throughout the ages to provide a path for the human race to follow back to God's presence. But all this knowledge would be mere rhetoric were it not for the Savior. Through sin man fell forever from God's kingdom, but through the Redeemer he has the opportunity to be saved.

The basis of the Law of Moses, and of all the principles, ordinances, and teachings of the gospel, both ancient and modern, is Jesus the Messiah. To help us recognize and accept him as the Son of God and the Savior of all mankind was the reason why the scriptures were preserved, and the parable of Lazarus and the rich man provides us with one of the most powerful witnesses ever given of the divinity of Jesus Christ.

Lazarus and the Rich Man

Luke 16:19–31

19. There was a certain rich man, which was clothed in purple and fine linen, and fared sumptuously every day:

20. And there was a

certain beggar named
Lazarus, which was laid at
his gate, full of sores,
21. And desiring to be
fed with the crumbs which
fell from the rich man's
table: moreover the dogs
came and licked his sores.
22. And it came to pass,
that the beggar died, and
was carried by the angels
into Abraham's bosom: the
rich man also died, and was
buried;
23. And in hell he lift up
his eyes, being in torments,
and seeth Abraham afar off,
and Lazarus in his bosom.
24. And he cried and
said, Father Abraham, have
mercy on me, and send
Lazarus, that he may dip the
tip of his finger in water,
and cool my tongue; for I
am tormented in this flame.
25. But Abraham said,
Son, remember that thou in
thy lifetime receivedst thy
good things, and likewise
Lazarus evil things: but now
he is comforted, and thou
art tormented.
26. And beside all this,
between us and you there is
a great gulf fixed: so that
they which would pass from
hence to you cannot; neither
can they pass to us, that
would come from thence.
27. Then he said, I pray
thee therefore, father, that
thou wouldest send him to
my father's house:
28. For I have five
brethren; that he may testify
unto them, lest they also
come into this place of
torment.
29. Abraham saith unto
him, They have Moses and
the prophets; let them hear
them.
30. And he said, Nay,
father Abraham: but if one
went unto them from the
dead, they will repent.
31. And he said unto
him, If they hear not Moses
and the prophets, neither
will they be persuaded,
though one rose from the
dead.

It is obvious from the scriptures that the Jewish leadership recognized the meaning of the parables of Jesus.[1] But even though they "perceived" that he spoke of them in his parables, they refused to abandon their errors and follow him. They earnestly looked for their Messiah, but they did not want Jesus to be him.

This parable was given by the Lord after the parable of the unjust steward,[2] wherein Christ enumerated specific instructions and admonitions pertaining to worldly things as related to the kingdom of God. The Pharisees had heard the parable and the admonitions, and "they derided him" because of them (Luke 16:14). In response to their derision Jesus said, "Ye are they which justify yourselves before men; but God knoweth your hearts: for that which is highly esteemed among men is abomination in the sight of God" (Luke 16:15).

The Pharisees and rulers were the keepers of the Mosaic Law, but they used the Law to justify their actions before men, allowed the Law to separate them from the people, and esteemed the praises of men more than the praises of God. They allowed their position and the things of the world to influence their ability to recognize the Messiah. As a result, the Messiah they anticipated was not the one who arrived. They had mistaken the signs and teachings of the Second Coming for those of the first. They were looking for the sign of the coming of the Son of Man, or the second coming of the Lord. The reasons for this centered around three specific situations:

The first was political in nature. The Jews had been in bondage for hundreds of years, and it was their belief that the coming Messiah would grant them freedom from this bondage.[3] He would destroy their enemies, rain down judgment and disaster upon the wicked, and punish with death and destruction those who oppressed Israel. Jesus, however, offered freedom not of the body, but of the soul. The intent of his coming was to establish his spiritual kingdom, not his earthly one. He did not promise freedom from bondage, but freedom from sin.[4]

But the Jews wanted an earthly king, not a spiritual one. This general expectation of both the leaders and the common people of Israel is confirmed by the reaction of the multitude in the miracle of the feeding of the five thousand.[5] In this miracle they wanted to force Jesus to be their king. They wanted his kingdom —but on the earth, not in heaven.

The second reason the Jews missed the Messiah involved the positions the leaders held. The scribes, Pharisees, and chief priests had developed into a religious ruling class. They had done this in an attempt to preserve the nation for the coming Messiah, but in so doing they had become so imbued with their own self-importance that they would not sacrifice their positions to accept their Savior.

The development of the teachings and doctrines of the Rabbinical Law had, over the centuries, elevated these leaders above the people they wanted to preserve. They denounced the sinner, the publican, the heathen, and the Sabbath breaker; they extolled the teacher, the rabbi, the Law, and the Pharisee. They cringed when Jesus ate with sinners and publicans, mingled with heathens, and offered the kingdom to all nations as he denounced the ruling class as hypocrites and whited sepulchres (Matthew 23:27). To accept him meant that they must serve rather than be served, they must give rather than receive, and must proclaim rather than be acclaimed.[6]

The third reason for missing the Savior evolved naturally from the previous two. It revolved around the things of the world. In the parable of the unjust steward (delivered just before this one) the Lord taught that there was no relationship between earthly things and the kingdom of God. Earthly things were of no eternal importance, and the acquisition of them bore no relationship to the attainment of salvation.

This concept was repugnant to the Pharisees and other leaders of the Jews. To accept Jesus as their Messiah meant denying all that they perceived as being important.[7] If they believed in him, they felt they would lose their leadership positions and the worldly things that they had accumulated; moreover, as a nation they would still be in political bondage.

Still, the teachings of Jesus, his miracles, and his claims to be the Messiah stirred their consciences and led them to earnestly seek from him a sign. On four recorded occasions they asked him to prove that he was the Savior:

1. After he had performed some of his miracles they requested signs of him (Matthew 12:38—40; Luke 11:16; John 2:18).

2. Prior to his sermon on the bread of life they asked him, "What sign shewest thou then, that we may see, and believe thee?" (John 6:30.)

3. The Pharisees and the Sadducees came tempting him and specifically requested "that he would shew them a sign from heaven" (Matthew 16:1).

4. They asked for a sign during the healing of the nobleman's son, and Jesus responded, "Except ye see signs and wonders, ye will not believe" (John 4:48).

The Lord received added insult during his trial when he was sent to Herod, who "hoped to have seen some miracle done by him" (Luke 23:8).

This attitude on the part of the Jews appears to be the reason for the parable of Lazarus and the rich man. It was a culminating parable that specifically pointed out the errors of the Pharisees and the rulers of the Jews. It was based on their erroneous belief that worldly wealth and attainment guaranteed them the kingdom (because they were the chosen people); further, it foretold the sign they had so longed to see. The parable was also given to denounce what the Law had become, to rebuke the Jews' disbelief in him, and to witness to the world that Jesus was the Messiah.

The first part of the parable was couched in a story that was common in the folklore of Judaism.[8] The two main characters were portrayed as being at opposite ends of the economic spectrum. There was a rich man who was clothed in purple and fine linen (symbolic of his wealth and royal position) who "fared sumptuously every day," meaning that he ate in abundance and only the best.

In opposition to this grandeur and worldly attainment (so highly esteemed by the Pharisees) was the other character of the parable—Lazarus. Lazarus was a beggar who lay at the rich man's gate and was full of sores. The affluent life-style of the rich man contrasted sharply with Lazarus's poverty. The beggar was reduced to eating the crumbs which fell from the rich man's table. It was the custom of wealthy Jews to use pieces of bread dipped in water as napkins. The bread was then discarded under the table, and later gathered up to be given to beggars and the poor.[9] With this and other garbage that came from the rich man's table, Lazarus tried to satisfy his needs. His physical condition was so deplorable that open sores covered his body, and dogs came and licked them.

Eventually both men died. The beggar was carried to Abraham's bosom, but the rich man went to hell. The Lord reversed the positions of Lazarus and the rich man to dramatize the relationship between earthly achievements and the kingdom of heaven. Lazarus was with the great patriarch Abraham, where every Jew longed to go. But the rich man, who had been so successful in acquiring material things on the earth, "in hell he lift up his eyes, being in torments."

The Lord now moved quickly to the next part of the parable. A discussion commenced between the rich man and Abraham. The rich man, realizing that his heavenly anticipations had not been fulfilled, asked Abraham to send Lazarus to comfort him and give him relief. "Send Lazarus," the rich man pleaded, "that he may dip the tip of his finger in water, and cool my tongue; for I am tormented in this flame." This was not a Dante's inferno; the rich man was in torment because of the comforts he had lost as a result of his selfish and unrepentant life.

Abraham quickly explained the differences between the two men. During his earthly life, the rich man had selfishly sought and acquired all the good things he wanted. Lazarus had received none of these comforts; but we assume his life was a righteous one, for he was allowed to enter into paradise at his death. His lack of accomplishment in the things of the world had not hindered his spiritual progress. The Pharisees would have thought Lazarus's earthly condition was a result of his sins and that he was being punished by God.[10] Lazarus's heavenly achievements would have surprised them, since the situation specifically contradicted their beliefs and practices.

Abraham explained to the rich man that there was a great gulf between him and Lazarus that could not be crossed. Many scholars of the past did not understand what this great gulf was.[11] Fortunately, because of the restoration of the gospel we are not left in darkness any longer concerning this phenomenon. It was the separation that existed at the time of the parable between paradise (the place where righteous and obedient children of the Father reside after death to await the resurrection) and the spirit prison (the place where disobedient children go to await, perchance, some grace or plan to come from God that would relieve them of their awful torment). That gulf would later be bridged by Jesus as he resided for a short time in the spirit world, after his death and before his resurrection.[12]

Having thus been instructed by Abraham, the rich man resigned himself to his own fate. But his conversation with Abraham continued as the Lord commenced teaching the most important doctrine of the parable. The rich man declared that he had five brothers. They were doing the same things that he had done, and he requested that Abraham send Lazarus to them that they might be told what their fate would be if they continued in their earthly ways. Abraham reminded the rich man that his brothers had "Moses and the prophets" to direct their lives.

The parable now reaches its climax. Jesus was instructing the covenant people, and rich or poor, they had had Moses and the prophets to teach them for hundreds of years. But the goal of this teaching had remained the same—recognition of the long-awaited Messiah and admission into the kingdom of God. Using Moses and the prophets, Jesus witnessed his divinity to the people. He had fulfilled the prophesies. "Search the scriptures," he said; "for in them ye think ye have eternal life: and they are they which testify of me" (John 5:39).

But the rich man in the parable wanted more: he wanted a sign. This was the same position the Pharisees were in, and the Lord told them that they had the same resources as the rich man—Moses and the prophets. But they, too, wanted more—they also wanted a sign.

Just as in the parable the rich man pleaded for Lazarus to be sent from the dead to warn his five brothers, the Pharisees wanted a sign from Christ to satisfy their doubts. As the parable drew to a close, Abraham informed the rich man that not even if one came from the dead would they (the brothers) change if they would not believe Moses and the prophets. This truth was vividly illustrated by the miracle of the raising of the nonfictional Lazarus.

The Miracle of the Raising of Lazarus[13]

John 11:1–44

1. Now a certain man was sick, named Lazarus, of Bethany, the town of Mary and her sister Martha.

2. (It was that Mary which anointed the Lord with ointment, and wiped his feet with her hair, whose brother Lazarus was sick.)

3. Therefore his sisters sent unto him, saying, Lord, behold, he whom thou lovest is sick.

4. When Jesus heard that, he said, This sickness is not unto death, but for the glory of God, that the Son of God might be glorified thereby.

5. Now Jesus loved Martha, and her sister, and Lazarus.

6. When he had heard therefore that he was sick, he abode two days still in the same place where he was.

7. Then after that saith he to his disciples, Let us go into Judaea again.

8. His disciples say unto him, Master, the Jews of late sought to stone thee; and goest thou thither again?

9. Jesus answered, Are there not twelve hours in the day? If any man walk in the day, he stumbleth not, because he seeth the light of this world.

10. But if a man walk in the night, he stumbleth, because there is no light in him.

11. These things said he: and after that he saith unto them, Our friend Lazarus sleepeth; but I go, that I may awake him out of sleep.

12. Then said his disciples, Lord, if he sleep, he shall do well.

13. Howbeit Jesus spake of his death: but they thought that he had spoken of taking of rest in sleep.

14. Then said Jesus unto them plainly, Lazarus is dead.

15. And I am glad for your sakes that I was not there, to the intent ye may believe; nevertheless let us go unto him.

16. Then said Thomas, which is called Didymus, unto his fellowdisciples, Let us also go, that we may die with him.

17. Then when Jesus came, he found that he had lain in the grave four days already.

18. Now Bethany was nigh unto Jerusalem, about fifteen furlongs off:

19. And many of the Jews came to Martha and Mary, to comfort them concerning their brother.

20. Then Martha, as soon as she heard that Jesus was coming, went and met him: but Mary sat still in the house.

21. Then said Martha unto Jesus, Lord, if thou hadst been here, my brother had not died.

22. But I know, that even now, whatsoever thou wilt ask of God, God will give it thee.

23. Jesus saith unto her, Thy brother shall rise again.

24. Martha saith unto him, I know that he shall rise again in the resurrection at the last day.

25. Jesus said unto her, I am the resurrection, and the life: he that believeth in me, though he were dead, yet shall he live:

26. And whosoever liveth and believeth in me shall never die. Believest thou this?

27. She saith unto him, Yea, Lord: I believe that thou art the Christ, the Son of God, which should come into the world.

28. And when she had so said, she went her way, and called Mary her sister secretly, saying, The Master is come, and calleth for thee.

29. As soon as she heard that, she arose quickly, and came unto him.

30. Now Jesus was not yet come into the town, but was in that place where Martha met him.

31. The Jews then which were with her in the house, and comforted her, when they saw Mary, that she rose up hastily and went out, followed her, saying, She goeth unto the grave to weep there.

32. Then when Mary was come where Jesus was, and saw him, she fell down at his feet, saying unto him, Lord, if thou hadst been here, my brother had not died.

33. When Jesus therefore saw her weeping, and the Jews also weeping which came with her, he groaned in the spirit, and was troubled,

34. And said, Where have ye laid him? They said unto him, Lord, come and see.

35. Jesus wept.

36. Then said the Jews, Behold how he loved him!

37. And some of them said, Could not this man, which opened the eyes of the blind, have caused that even this man should not have died?

38. Jesus therefore again groaning in himself cometh to the grave. It was a cave, and a stone lay upon it.

39. Jesus said, Take ye away the stone. Martha, the sister of him that was dead, saith unto him, Lord, by this time he stinketh: for he hath been dead four days.

40. Jesus saith unto her, Said I not unto thee, that, if thou wouldest believe, thou shouldest see the glory of God?

41. Then they took away the stone from the place where the dead was laid. And Jesus lifted up his eyes, and said, Father, I thank thee that thou hast heard me.

42. And I knew that thou hearest me always: but because of the people which stand by I said it, that they may believe that thou hast sent me.

43. And when he thus had spoken, he cried with a loud voice, Lazarus, come forth.

44. And he that was dead came forth, bound hand and foot with grave-

clothes: and his face was bound about with a napkin. Jesus saith unto them, Loose him, and let him go.

Lazarus was the brother of Mary and Martha, and they lived in Bethany. They were close friends of the Lord. When Lazarus became ill his sisters sent a message to Jesus declaring, "Lord, behold, he whom thou lovest is sick." Jesus received the message and declared that the sickness was not unto death, but that "the Son of God might be glorified thereby." He remained two days where he was and then told his Apostles that he would go again into Judea. They cautioned him because of the antagonism toward him there, but Jesus was intent on going. He told them that Lazarus was asleep and he would go and awaken him.

The disciples misunderstood, thinking that the sleep would benefit Lazarus. But Jesus would not have this miracle misunderstood, and he openly declared to them, "Lazarus is dead." They then proceeded back to Bethany and found that Lazarus had been in the grave for four days.

Mary and Martha went separately to Jesus as he approached Bethany. Each voiced her concern that he had not come in time to save Lazarus, and Martha acknowledged that "even now, whatsoever thou wilt ask of God, God will give it thee." Jesus reminded her of who he was and told her that Lazarus would rise again. She acknowledged Christ, and agreed that Lazarus would rise in the resurrection. But she misunderstood the Lord's intentions, so he openly declared to her, "I am the resurrection, and the life: he that believeth in me, though he were dead, yet shall he live." He asked if she believed this, and she again acknowledged him as the Messiah.

Mary and Martha were not alone at this time, for many of the Jews from Jerusalem and its environs were with the sisters in their hour of grief. The family was well known, and their popularity might have been enhanced by their association with Jesus. Fellow disciples would have given the family comfort, and disbelievers and enemies may have been there in anticipation of Jesus' arrival so that they could again accuse him. Regardless of their motivation many people would have been with Mary and Martha, for one of the most binding of the Jewish directives was "to obey the Rabbinic direction of accompanying the dead, so as to show honour to the departed and kindness to the survivors."[14]

The sequence of events that then took place is fundamental to the purpose of both the miracle and the parable. Mary and Martha and the other mourners approached Jesus, and the scripture reports that Jesus groaned in the spirit and was troubled. He was undoubtedly affected by the intense sorrow displayed at the physical death of Lazarus. But this was the Savior, he who took upon himself all sorrows. Isaiah had declared centuries before that he was "a man of sorrows, and acquainted with grief. . . . Surely he hath borne our griefs, and carried our sorrows" (Isaiah 53:3–4). But he was also troubled—for even those who believed in him did not fully understand his power.

Jesus wept, and asked where they had laid Lazarus. This visual show of emotion caused mixed feelings among the crowd. Some assumed that it was due to his grief for Lazarus, and noted how he loved him. Others, with rancor in their hearts, questioned why he had allowed such a friend to die. Jesus wept not only for the genuine sorrow of his friends, but for the disbelief and mockery of his enemies.

Christ arrived at the tomb (a cave with a large stone sealing its entrance) and asked that the stone be removed. Martha's response was logical. "Lord, by this time he stinketh: for he hath been dead four days." She still did not understand what was happening, and Jesus chided her. "Said I not unto thee, that, if thou wouldest believe, thou shouldest see the glory of God?" The stone was rolled away and Jesus lifted up his eyes and said, "Father, I thank thee that thou hast heard me. And I knew that thou hearest me always: but because of the people which stand by I said it, that they may believe that thou hast sent me."

The crowd was observing all that the Lord did, and they must have been astonished at the opening of the tomb. Christ had twice before openly declared the purpose of this miracle and now, before the entire crowd—friends and enemies alike—he openly declared it again. His enemies had asked him for a sign many times and he had refused them on each of those occasions. But now he would give them a sign that they could not forget. "Lazarus, come forth," he cried with a loud voice, so that all might hear; and Lazarus came forth!

John reports that many of the Jews believed on Christ, but there were others who "went their ways to the Pharisees, and told them what things Jesus had done." These same Pharisees had stood before Jesus as he gave them the parable that declared his divinity, but now they gathered a council, for in their minds the very root of the tree of their authority was endangered. "What do we," they said, "if we let him thus alone, all men will believe on him." Then they revealed the real reason for their concern (and fulfilled the teaching of the parable) when they said, "The Romans shall come and take away both our place and nation."

They were not concerned whether Jesus was or was not the Messiah. They were like the rich man of the parable, concerned only with the things of the world, their existence as a nation, and their personal prominence among the people. Caiaphas stepped forward and unwittingly acknowledged the Messiah's mission when he declared, "It is expedient for us, that one man should die for the people, and that the whole nation perish not" (John 11:46–50). Jesus would die for all, not to save the nation, but to save the souls of all those who would follow him and live his commandments.

From that moment on Christ's fate was sealed. It was no longer a question of *if* the Jewish leaders would kill him, but *when* and *how.* Even Lazarus was in jeopardy, for John records that after the miracle, many of the Jews counseled that they might also put him to death (John 12:10).

In the parable of Lazarus and the rich man, Abraham told the rich man that if his five brethren would not listen to Moses and the prophets, they would not be persuaded to repent even if one rose from the dead. The actions of the Jewish leadership after the raising of Lazarus proved that this was true. They made a mockery of the Law and, as prophesied in the parable, they did not believe, "though one rose from the dead."

The Jews asked Christ to give them a sign of his Messiahship, and he raised Lazarus from the dead in fulfillment of parabolic prophecy. Yet they denied this perfect witness. They sought to preserve a nation, but the very man who could insure its deliverance they rejected.

Part Seven

The Message of the Parables

As It Was Then, So It Is Today 12

The parables of Jesus were stories of everyday life, teaching tools that encompassed the marvelous truths of the kingdom of heaven. Although only a small portion of Christ's life is detailed in the New Testament Gospels, from the parables we know that he was familiar with every aspect of life, and he used that great knowledge to illustrate his teachings.

As the people stood before him and listened to his discourses they heard his verbal claim to the Messiahship, and they could see in his miracles the power of his divinity. But in his parables they heard simple stories of life, stories that used everyday activities to teach eternal truths.

They could think about the gospel and their responsibility within it as they sowed in their fields or mixed leaven into their bread. They could relate to the joy of finding treasure, either sought for or inadvertently discovered. And as they tended their sheep or put their money to the exchangers, they could again remember the eternal principles He had taught.

Jesus taught the people of prayer, obedience, forgiveness, and mercy. He taught eternal relationships through the two great commandments. His people were to love and care for each other, to live in the world but not be a part of it, and to give their eternal devotion to God. Their selfish limitations were expanded and their limited vision enlarged. The exactness of the Mosaic Law had helped them to determine who their neighbor was; the gospel's second great commandment required them to review in their hearts, "Whose neighbor am I?"

Through talents, pounds, and vineyards the Lord taught accountability and reward for laboring in the kingdom, yet he couched warnings in the stories of the foolish rich man and the prayers of the Pharisee and the publican. All this he taught to impress upon the minds of his Father's children that the things of the world bore no relationship to the kingdom of God.

He taught the Jews of their impending judgment, and reminded them that their chosen position was in jeopardy when he said, "Of stones God could raise up children unto Abraham." He compared the rulers of Israel to the husbandmen of a vineyard, and declared that their eventual judgment would be based on how they tended that vineyard.

Through their ceremony and celebration of marriage he warned the covenant people that to be invited to the festivities was one thing, to accept the invitation was another, but to eat with the King of heaven required much more.

Henceforth when fishermen who had heard his parables threw their nets into the sea, drew forth fish, and separated the good from the bad, they would be reminded of the eternal judgment that they faced. The solemn warning given to the Church was that mere membership, just being under the auspices of the covenant, would not guarantee entrance into the Lord's kingdom.

Agonized by his verbal claims, his miracles, and his very presence, the Jewish leadership sought a sign from Christ to confirm his Messiahship. He would not show his power when they demanded it, but through the parable of Lazarus and the rich man, he prophesied of the "sign's" coming, and finally fulfilled their incessant desire for a sign with the miracle of the raising of Lazarus.

For the most part, the chosen people understood the parables and applied them correctly. Some believed and followed the Savior, seeking additional guidance so that they might enter his kingdom. Others openly rejected him, refusing to give up their social or political positions and the rich things of the world. Ultimately, the Jewish leaders gathered together and discussed how they might entrap him in his words and destroy him.

The parables had specific meaning for the Jews of Christ's time, yet their impact has extended forward, applying not only to our day, but to the future as well. Although times have changed, the stories were so simply and beautifully given that it requires little imagination to apply the principles encased within them.

The impact of the parables in our day is the same as in days of old. Some people hear the Savior's voice and accept of his knowledge and love, striving to be lifted up to the Father's kingdom. But others disbelieve and reject the Lord's principles—sometimes seeking additional ways to destroy him. The Carpenter from Nazareth tried in many ways to teach the gospel, and his powerful message is clearly portrayed in the parables of Jesus the Messiah.

Notes

Introduction

1. Miracles, chapter 1.

2. See chapter 1, note 26.

3. Bruce p. viii.

4. The determination of which of the teachings of Jesus should be classified as parables has varied throughout the years depending on how strictly the word *parable* is defined. As few as twenty-seven (Siegfried Goebel, *The Parables of Jesus,* 1883, p. 3) or as many as fifty-three (A. Julicher, *Die Gleichnisreden Jesu,* 1910, p. 15) or even sixty-five (Francis L. Filas, *The Parables of Jesus,* 1959) have been so determined.

5. Farrar 1:325.

Chapter 1: Parables

1. Bible Dictionary, "Parables."

2. Geikie 2:144.

3. Dodd p. 4; Ed 1:580.

4. Trench p. 4; EB, myth.

5. JC p. 298; EB, fable.

6. Trench p. 4; EB, proverb.

7. JC p. 299; Trench p. 5; EB, allegory.

8. JC p. 298.

9. JC p. 296; Ed 1:580; Barclay pp. 9—11.

10. Ed 1:581.

11. Geikie 2:145.

12. Chapter 2.

13. Further proof of the leadership's understanding is evidenced by the Synoptics' report that the leaders held councils against the Lord (Matthew 12:14), watched him (Luke 20:20), tried to catch him in his words (Mark 12:13), and contrived arguments against his claim (Matthew 12:24).

14. Chapter 10.

15. Chapter 10.

16. Bruce p. 310.

17. PM p. 511.

18. Geikie 2:146.

19. JC p. 297.

20. Ed 1:584.

21. Dodd p. 161.

22. Ed 1:145.

23. Ed 2:55.

24. Ed 1:544; Trench p. 13; Bruce p. ix, 313; Filas p. 4.

25. Miracles, chapter 1.

26. The church of the Middle Ages interpreted the parables allegorically; every word, person, event, and detail of the parables had a secret inner meaning. One example is Augustine's interpretation of the parable of the good Samaritan:

"*A certain man went down from Jerusalem to Jericho:* Adam himself is meant; *Jerusalem* is the heavenly city of peace, from whose blessedness Adam fell; *Jericho* means the moon, and signifies our mortality, because it is born, waxes, wanes, and dies. *Thieves* are the devil and his angels. *Who stripped him,* namely, of his immortality; *and beat him,* by persuading him to sin; *and left him half-dead,* because in so far as man can understand and know God, he lives, but in so far as he is wasted and oppressed by sin, he is dead; he is therefore called *half-dead.* The *priest* and *Levite* who saw him and passed by, signify the priesthood and ministry of the Old Testament, which could profit nothing for salvation. *Samaritan* means Guardian, and therefore the Lord Himself is signified by this name. The *binding of the wounds* is the restraint of sin. *Oil* is the comfort of good hope; *wine* the exhortation to work with fervent spirit. The *beast* is the flesh in which He deigned to come to us. The being *set upon the beast* is belief in the incarnation of Christ. The *inn* is the Church, where travellers returning to their heavenly country are refreshed after pilgrimage. The *morrow* is after the resurrection of the Lord. The *two pence* are either the two precepts of love, or the promise of this life and of that which is to come. The *innkeeper* is the Apostle (Paul). The supererogatory payment is either his counsel of celibacy, or the fact that he worked with his own hands lest he should be a burden to any of the weaker brethren when the Gospel was new, though it was lawful for him 'to live by the Gospel.' (*Quaestiones Evangeliorum,* II. 19—slightly abridged.)" (As quoted in Dodd pp. 1–2.)

Clearly erroneous, this concept was cast aside as the Reformists developed their own methods of interpretation which also led to embellishment by the teacher or translator. (Jeremias p. 89.)

27. JC p. 286.

28. Trench p. 15.

Chapter 2: The Gospel's Inherent Strength

1. It is most unlikely that Jesus actually delivered seven or eight parables on this singular occasion. It is more likely that Matthew simply chose to record the seven parables together, that he might deliver them to the saints for their edification. Farrar p. 323.

2. In an effort to counter the effect of the many miracles of Jesus, the leadership of the Jews accused him of performing them by the power of Beelzebub, the prince of devils. This argument undoubtedly had a damaging effect upon the people's belief in Christ, for it gave them an alternative to believe in. For further detail see Miracles, chapter 3.

3. Ed 1:586–87.

4. DNTC 1:288.

5. HC 2:266.

6. Trench p. 31.

7. Buttrick p. 46.

8. Trench p. 31.

9. MM 2:252.

10. DNTC 1:288.

11. DNTC 1:289.

12. Dodd p. 148.

13. Ed 1:590.

14. For example: the pearl of great price, the lost coin, the sower, the ten virgins, the great supper, labourers in the vineyard.

15. Jeremias p. 101.

16. DNTC 1:296.

17. TPJS pp. 97–98; DNTC 1:296–97.

18. Trench p. 35; Ed 1:589.

19. HC 2:181–200, HC (Index) Apostles.

20. Trench p. 36.

21. MM 2:257.

22. JC p. 287.

23. MM 2:258–59.

24. TPJS p. 101.

25. MF p. 303.

26. JC p. 290.

27. Ed 1:592.

28. Jeremias p. 147.

29. Ed 1:592.

30. DNTC 1:298.

31. JC p. 291.

32. TPJS pp. 98–99.

33. Ed 1:594.

34. JC p. 291.

35. DNTC 1:299.

36. HC 5:207.

37. HC 2:270.
38. Ed 1:588.
39. DNTC 1:292.

Chapter 3: The Gospel Once Discovered

1. Ed 1:595–96.
2. Jeremias p. 198.
3. JC p. 293.
4. MM 2:265.
5. An interesting modern application was made of this parable by Joseph Smith. He applied it to the gathering of the Church. He said, "See the Church of the Latter-day Saints, selling all that they have, and gathering themselves together unto a place that they may purchase for an inheritance, that they may be together and bear each other's afflictions in the day of calamity" (HC 2:272).
6. See chapter 2, notes 14, 15.
7. Trench p. 49.
8. MM 2:264.
9. JC p. 294.
10. Joseph Smith applied the parable to the early members of the Church as follows: "The Saints again work after this example. See men traveling to find places for Zion and her stakes or remnants, who, when they find the place for Zion, or the pearl of great price, straightway sell that they have, and buy it." (HC 2:272.)

Chapter 4: Lost and Then Found

1. Geikie 2:328.
2. Trench p. 133.
3. JC p. 454–55.
4. Trench p. 133.
5. JC p. 455.
6. HC 5:261–62.
7. MM 3:246.
8. Ed 2:256.
9. JC p. 456.
10. JC p. 456.
11. Ed 2:257.

12. When Joseph Smith was asked his opinion of the parable of the prodigal son, he stated: "The Elders of this Church have preached largely upon it, without having any rule of interpretation." He continued and asked the question, "What is the rule of interpretation? Just no interpretation at all. Understand it precisely as it reads." (HC 5:261.)

13. Trench p. 143.

14. MF p. 307.

15. JC p. 461.

16. MF p. 307.

17. Smith, p. 21.

18. DNTC 1:510–12.

Chapter 5: Teaching Gospel Principles

1. Bruce p. 158.
2. JC p. 436.
3. Bruce p. 159.
4. JC p. 436.
5. DNTC 1:542.
6. Ed 2:285.
7. DNTC 1:542.
8. Trench p. 178.
9. Miracles, chapter 9.

10. This parable was used by the Lord to admonish the persecuted Saints in the early history of the restored church. During the Missouri period the persecutions were unusually severe, ending with the Saints' expulsion from Missouri under the extermination order of Governor Boggs (HC 3:175, 426). These Saints, called the "children of Zion" by the Lord, were likened to the "parable of the woman and the unjust judge." After quoting the parable, the Lord admonished the Saints to petition all forms of government for the deserved redress, with the comforting conclusion that if the seats of government did not heed them then the Lord would "arise and come forth out of his hiding place, and in his fury vex the nation" (D&C 101:81–94).

11. Ed 2:240.

12. Ed(JSL) pp. 47–49; Ed 2:240.

13. JC p. 435.

14. Ed 2:241.

15. JC p. 435.

16. Farrar p. 453.

17. An interesting experience in the history of the Church also illustrates this need for continuous righteous petitioning. During the Missouri persecutions Joseph Smith was commanded by the Lord to organize companies of the

members to go to Missouri for the redemption of Zion. The Lord admonished Joseph and the early brethren to pray earnestly and seek diligently to obtain his will. The Lord desired five hundred men to go up to redeem Zion but recognized that man would not always do his will. He therefore admonished them to seek for three hundred, or no less than one hundred (D&C 103). By this order Zion's Camp was organized for the redemption of Zion (HC 2:61–83).

18. Geikie 2:296.

19. Miracles, chapter 15.

20. Geikie 2:384.

21. JC p. 532; Ed 2:422.

22. Geikie 2:384.

23. MF pp. 95–96.

24. Ed 1:564.

25. JC p. 261.

26. Ed 1:564.

27. Bruce pp. 238–39.

28. Ed 1:564.

29. Trench p. 104.

30. JC p. 263; Ed 1:563.

31. Ed 1:563.

32. Ed 1:561.

33. A similar recording was given of the two cleansings of the temple: one at the beginning of Christ's ministry (John 2:13–25), and one at its close (Matthew 21:12–13).

34. JC p. 262.

35. Chapter 4.

36. Bruce p. 401.

37. Trench p. 55.

38. Trench p. 55.

39. DNTC 1:429.

40. JC p. 394.

41. Josephus records that Archelaus received tribute from Perea, Galilee, Idumea, Judea, Samaria, and certain cities including Jerusalem: the annual sum was six hundred talents. (*Antiquities*, Book XVII, XI, 4) Although the sum may vary depending on the talent used to calculate it, it was not the intent of the parable to declare an exact amount due, but to convey the reality of such an enormous amount that repayment was hopeless.

42. Ed 2:293.

43. JC p. 395.

44. Ed 2:296.

45. FPM pp. 193–94.

46. MF p. 59.
47. MF p. 269.

Chapter 6: Teaching Relationships

1. Ed 2:306.
2. JC p. 469.
3. Bruce p. 170.
4. Geikie 2:339.
5. JC p. 470.
6. JC p. 470.
7. Central to Luke's theme on the uses and abuses of worldly wealth, in addition to this parable, are the parables of the prodigal son and Lazarus and the rich man. In addition, he records the discussion between Jesus and the rich young ruler (Luke 18:18–25; see also Matthew 19:16–29; Mark 10:17–30). Luke continues this theme connecting the parables of the unjust steward and Lazarus and the rich man with additional verses on worldly possessions (Luke 16:10–16). Although these topics are sequential in Luke chapter 16, they are widely dispersed in Matthew. Luke 16:10 is only referred to in Matthew 25:21 in association with the reward of the parable of the talents; verses 11 and 12 have no parallel in the Gospels; verse 13 appears in Matthew 6:24. In verses 14 and 15 the Lord applied the teachings of the parable to the Pharisees; the only comparable reference is his comment in Matthew 23:14 on "devour[ing] widows' houses," a reference, it would seem, to their greediness. Verse 16 appears in Matthew 11:12–13; verse 17 in Matthew 5:18; and verse 18 in Matthew 5:32.
8. Geikie 2:333.
9. Ed 2:339.
10. Farrar 2:125.
11. Ed 2:266.
12. Trench p. 154.
13. JC p. 464.
14. JC p. 463.
15. Jeremias p. 182.
16. DNTC 1:513.
17. JC p. 464.
18. Chapter 5.
19. Geikie 2:318.
20. Miracles, chapter 6.
21. Ed 2:303–4.
22. DNTC 1:500.

Chapter 7: The Second Great Commandment

1. Ed 2:234; Trench p. 109. The scriptures record several examples of questions being posed to Jesus, with both good and evil intentions. Mark reports that upon one occasion the Pharisees and Herodians specifically sent people to the Savior to "catch him in his words" (Mark 12:13). Luke reports that after a particularly strong denunciation of the rulers of the Jews, the scribes and Pharisees again began to "urge him vehemently, and to provoke him to speak many things: lying wait for him and seeking to catch something out of his mouth, that they might accuse him" (Luke 11:53–54).

Luke, in the good Samaritan parable, does not impute the antagonism to the questioner as specifically noted in the other examples. (Matthew and Mark report a similar instance, perhaps the same as that of Luke, but without the parable (Mark 12:28–34; Matthew 22:35–40). It could therefore be concluded that the phrase *tempting him* could properly mean "to make trial of," or that he would "make proof of" the skill of Jesus. (Trench p. 109.)

An example of this type of meaning is found in Genesis, where God "tempts" Abraham in the story of the proposed sacrifice of Isaac (Genesis 22:1). God did not "tempt" Abraham in the evil sense of the word; but put him to proof, trying his faith by the means described in the story. James, in the New Testament, supports this interpretation, assuming the successful overcoming of the trial, when he states, "Blessed is the man that endureth temptation: for when he is tried, he shall receive the crown of life" (James 1:12).

2. JC p. 430. Perhaps we should be grateful to the lawyer for the question, since it elicited such a memorable response.
3. Ed 2:234–35.
4. Barnett pp. 79–80.
5. Ed 2:237.
6. JC pp. 430–31.
7. Ed 2:239.
8. Ed 2:237.
9. Ed 2:238.
10. Jeremias p. 204; Geikie 2:295.
11. Trench p. 111.
12. Trench p. 114.
13. Ed 2:239; DNTC 1:471.

Chapter 8: Parables That Teach Accountability and Reward

1. Jeremias p. 63.
2. The parables of the pounds and the labourers in the vineyard.
3. Chapter 9.
4. MF pp. 100–101.

5. Trench p. 93.
6. Ed 2:459; Bruce p. 210.
7. JC pp. 583–84; Ed 2:463.
8. Bruce p. 205.
9. JC p. 583.
10. JC pp. 582–83.
11. HC 2:24; MF pp. 100–101.
12. Ed 2:464.
13. Ed 2:466.
14. Geikie 2:366; Josephus, Antiquities XVII, IX, 1; XVII, XI, 2.
15. DNTC 1:573.
16. Ed 2:466.
17. Trench p. 186.
18. JC pp. 509–10.
19. DNTC 1:572.
20. DNTC 1:573.
21. JC p. 510.
22. JC p. 509.
23. DNTC 1:572.
24. DNTC 1:571; JC p. 508.
25. Geikie 2:357.
26. JC p. 482.
27. Ed 2:416.
28. Ed 2:417–18.
29. DNTC 1:561; Trench p. 65.
30. Trench p. 63.
31. Farrar p. 504, as quoted in MM 3:307.
32. Farrar 2:164.
33. Ed 2:416.
34. See Bruce R. McConkie, *A New Witness for the Articles of Faith* (Salt Lake City: Deseret Book, 1985), pp. 149–51. See also: Philippians 2:12; 2 Nephi 10:24; 25:25; 3 Nephi 27:19; Moses 1:6; TG, Grace.

Chapter 9: Parables That Teach Warnings

1. The introduction in Luke 12:1 is unique to Luke, but the last part of verse 1 is found in Matthew 16:6, 12; and Mark 8:15. Verses 2–9 of Luke associate with Matthew 10:26–33, verse 9 also to Mark 8:38, verse 10 to Matthew 12:32; Mark 3:29, verse 12 to Matthew 10:19–20; Mark 13:11. Verses 13–21 cover the parable discussed, which is unique to Luke. Verses 22–34 appear in Matthew as part of the Sermon on the Mount, 6:25–30,

19–21. Verses 35–59 relate to Matthew 24:43–51; 10:34–36; 16:2–3; 5:25–26.

2. Ed 2:243.

3. Ed 2:243.

4. JC p. 439.

5. Trench p. 118.

6. JC p. 439.

7. MF p. 140.

8. Jeremias p. 165.

9. JC p. 440.

10. Ed 2:245.

11. Farrar 1:463.

12. JC p. 472.

13. JC p. 472.

14. Geikie 2:346.

15. Ed (Temple) p. 338.

16. Ed 1:311–13; 2:290–91.

17. Jeremias p. 143.

18. DNTC 1:543.

19. JC p. 473.

20. This was because the nation as a whole had given itself up in anticipation of a political Messiah who would free them from their earthly problems. See Geikie 2:167.

21. Ed 2:247.

22. Trench p. 123.

23. Ed 2:247.

24. DNTC 1:477.

Chapter 10: Parables That Teach Judgment

1. Matthew records that Jesus delivered the parable of the two sons first (see chapter 5 herein) and then gave this parable. Mark and Luke record that he taught the parable directly after the discussion on John's authority, leaving out the parable of the two sons.

2. DNTC 1:593.

3. JC p. 535.

4. MM 3:361.

5. DNTC 1:593; JC p. 534.

6. Ed 2:423–24.

7. MM 3:361.

8. Bruce p. 453.
9. Farrar 2:223–24.
10. Miracles, chapter 6.
11. Chapter 6.
12. Ed 2:249.
13. JC p. 538.
14. JC p. 451; DNTC 1:501.
15. JC p. 452.
16. Trench p. 129.
17. Ed 2:250.
18. JC p. 452; Ed 2:251.
19. Geikie 2:323.
20. See the parable of the Pharisee and publican, chapter 9 herein.
21. Ed 2:425–26.
22. DNTC 1:598.
23. JC p. 540.
24. This relationship is used many times in New Testament teachings (drawing upon the Old Testament for examples). All of the children of Israel that went out of Egypt were called, but not all were chosen to enter the promised land (1 Corinthians 10:1–10; Hebrews 3:7–19). Other examples might include that of the spies from the children of Israel that were originally sent into the promised land to spy it out for occupation; of them only Caleb and Joshua were chosen to actually enter therein (Numbers 13, 14). Of the twenty-two thousand assembled by Gideon to repel the army of the Midianites, God chose only three hundred to perform the task (Judges 7).
25. Geikie 2:390.
26. Ed 2:195 et seq; 248.
27. Trench p. 52.
28. MM 2:266.
29. JC p. 295.
30. MF pp. 304–5.
31. Joseph Smith summarized the parable in this manner: "For the work of this pattern, behold the seed of Joseph, spreading forth the Gospel net upon the face of the earth, gathering of every kind, that the good may be saved in vessels prepared for that purpose, and the angels will take care of the bad. So shall it be at the end of the world—the angels shall come forth and sever the wicked from among the just, and cast them into the furnace of fire, and there shall be wailing and gnashing of teeth." (HC 2:272.)
32. JC p. 576; MF p. 366.
33. Ed 1:354.
34. Ed 2:455.
35. Trench p. 85.
36. JC p. 579; FPM p. 253.

37. FPM p. 253–54.

38. See the parable of the sower, chapter 2 herein.

39. JC p. 579.

40. JC p. 579.

41. FPM p. 256.

42. FPM p. 254.

43. Chapter 8.

44. Chapter 9.

45. JC p. 579.

46. Ed 2:457.

47. FPM p. 256.

48. Tennyson pp. 228–29.

49. Trench p. 90.

50. MF p. 366.

Chapter 11: They Ask of Him a Sign

1. Chapter 1.

2. Chapter 6.

3. Ed 1:168–79.

4. Miracles, chapters 1, 10.

5. Miracles, chapter 2.

6. Ed 1:167, 308–35.

7. Ed 2:275–77.

8. Jeremias p. 182.

9. Jeremias p. 184.

10. Jeremias p. 185.

11. This phrase (the great gulf) has perplexed interpreters and scholars of the past, leaving them to declare openly that they did not know its meaning (Trench p. 168); or that it meant God's judgment was irrevocable (Jeremias p. 186).

12. Jesus did not personally go to the prison, for those that were there could not abide his presence. But he opened the way that others from paradise might pass over and teach the gospel to those in the prison that perchance they might, through diligence, repentance, and the grace of God, extricate themselves from that awful condition. (See further D&C 138.)

13. Miracles, chapter 10.

14. Ed 2:317.

Subject Index

— I —

— J —

— K —

— L —

— M —

— N —

Scripture Index

OLD TESTAMENT

NEW TESTAMENT

BOOK OF MORMON

DOCTRINE AND COVENANTS

PEARL OF GREAT PRICE